Your BABY FOOD Book

Your BABY FOOD Book

BY VIRGINIA DEMOSS

ANDERSON WORLD
BOOKS, INC.

Library of Congress Cataloging in Publication Data

DeMoss, Virginia, 1948-
  Your baby food book.

  1. Infants — Nutrition. 2. Children — Nutrition.
3. Pregnancy — Nutritional aspects. I. Title.
RJ216.D387 1984   649'.3   83-25668
ISBN 0-89037-289-6

Cover photography by David Keith
Book design by Kevin J. Moran
Photos on pg. 57, 74, 85, 140 and 161 are by the author.
All other photos are by Rebecca Colligan.

Anderson World Books, Inc.
1400 Stierlin Rd., Mountain View, CA 94043

CONTENTS

DEDICATION _____ 7

FOREWORD _____ 9

1: PREPARING FOR PREGNANCY _____ 11

2: HEALTHY HABITS FOR LIFE _____ 13

3: EATING RIGHT DURING PREGNANCY _____ 31

4: BREAST-FEED YOUR BABY _____ 55

5: BOTTLE-FEED YOUR BABY _____ 73

6: FROM BREAST TO SPOON _____ 81

7: BABY'S FIRST FOOD _____ 87

8: MOVING UP TO LUMPS AND CHUNKS _____ 109

9: TIME FOR TABLE FOOD _____ 121

10: FEEDING A SICK CHILD _____ 167

11: AN UPHILL BATTLE _____ 177

12: POSTPARTUM: THE FOURTH TRIMESTER __ 191

BIBLIOGRAPHY _____ 203

To Lael and Aaron: Eat your vegetables.

To Jane Brody for putting sanity and sense back into nutrition, and to Frances Moore Lappe and the dedicated people of the Center For Science In The Public Interest for giving it a conscience.

FOREWORD

You've picked up this book, so chances are you're one of today's "concerned parents." We read books to find out how to get pregnant (most efficiently), how to be pregnant (most conscientiously), how to have babies (most naturally) and how to raise children (most lovingly). I'm entitled to gloat, because I've done it all. Fortunately for my son and me, I no longer have time to read six books on each phase of our life together, so life post-partum is, in some ways, less intense.

I am certainly aware of the need for advice and direction for us new parents embarking on a life of child rearing. One of our main concerns is proper nutrition for our infants and children — what, when and how to feed for greatest benefit. Those of us who have had weight problems are especially concerned about passing on a legacy of compulsive eating to our children. We are aware of methods to control excess in the diet, but may be unsure of how to implement these ideas in our own and our children's lives.

Your Baby Food Book offers valuable information on nutrition for both children and adults based on the most recent recommendations of such institutions as the American Heart Association. You will also read practical and helpful advice for handling problems like, for example, what to feed a sick child.

9

There are sample recipes and menus as well as a list of reliable sources to consult. I find that *Your Baby Food Book* contains the same attention to detail and careful research that have characterized the author's work during the several years that I have reviewed her writing. *Your Baby Food Book* will complement your doctor's advice and help you add variety and nutrition to your child's diet.

It's easy to lose perspective on your eating patterns and their relative importance in life, especially when reading a book devoted to eating behaviors. It would be a good idea to read the conclusion of this book first; it will help you put eating (and feeding) in perspective. Eating is an important facet of your child's life, but only one facet. You should be concerned, not paranoid.

Good reading, and *bon appetit* to your children.

Carol Grimes
Professor, Chemistry and Nutrition
Golden West College
Huntington Beach, California

PREPARING FOR PREGNANCY

If you're still just thinking about having a baby you're reading this book at precisely the right time. The mother's job of properly nourishing her unborn child begins long before she becomes pregnant. If the mother has been eating a well-balanced diet and her weight is normal before conception, her chances of giving birth to a healthy baby are very good. On the other hand, if she is extremely undernourished, a woman may find it difficult to become pregnant in the first place.

The first priority for both parents is to get on the right nutritional track to provide a healthy, happy life for yourselves and your baby. Although the father won't be nourishing the baby during pregnancy and nursing, good nutrition is as important for him as for the mother. He can reinforce her good eating habits and take more responsibility for meal planning and preparation during the often exhausting periods of pregnancy and breast-feeding. Good nutrition will also allow him to live long enough to watch baby mature into adulthood. What's more, in today's more equitable living arrangements, it's likely — or should be — that dad will have as much hand as mom in feeding once baby has left the breast.

The best way to teach your child lifelong good eating habits is to follow them yourselves. It isn't likely you're going to spend 18 years or so preparing one type of meal for yourselves and another "healthy" one for junior. Besides, it's a rare youngster who will sit patiently eating broccoli and brussels sprouts while the adults have "the good stuff."

Adopting a good diet now is an excellent idea for a number of reasons. First, the sooner you begin, the sooner you will see improvements in your own health and well-being. Secondly, healthy eating habits will be second nature to you when it comes time to feed your own youngster. If you raise him on good habits, you won't have to break bad ones later.

The following chapter outlines a nutritional plan that can benefit you and your youngster. Now is the time for both of you to begin eating right, to lose weight if you need to and undertake an exercise program you can live with the rest of your lives.

How much do your eating and exercise habits influence your child? Consider these findings of a committee of the American Academy of Pediatrics:

"Fatness as well as leanness runs along family lines. When both parents are obese, the children tend to be obese. When both parents are lean, the children tend to be lean.

"Comparing the children of the obese with the children of the lean, we are impressed both by how fat the children of the obese are, and how fast they gain in fatness. By age 17, the children of two obese parents are three times as fat as the children of two lean parents!"

Furthermore, researchers have found that family obesity is based less on genetic factors than on "pseudo-heredity": Obese individuals tend to marry one another, reinforce shared attitudes toward food, eating, and exercise, and pass them along to their offspring. And to underscore even more dramatically the father's role in his children's health and well-being, the researchers found that when it comes to influencing children toward obesity, an obese father has more influence than an obese mother!

So, if you are like the average person, undoubtedly you have bad habits (smoking, drinking too much, eating in excess or eating the wrong things) that you've not yet been motivated to break. This could be a golden opportunity for you. . .and for your child. Knowing that minor alterations in your way of life can add immeasurably to your own health and to that of a new human being may be just the incentive you need. There was never a better time to begin.

HEALTHY HABITS FOR LIFE

Eating used to be a lot easier in the good old days when we didn't know any better. Breakfast was bacon, eggs, toast and coffee. Lunch was a burger and fries or a bologna and cheese sandwich with potato chips, a soda and cookies. Dinner wasn't dinner unless it consisted of meat, potatoes, a limp vegetable from a can, two slices of white bread and ice cream for dessert. Nutrition was as easy as the "Basic Four Food Groups" (meat, dairy, breads and cereals, fruits and vegetables, in order of importance); it didn't matter what we ate from those groups or how it was prepared as long as representatives of each found their way onto the plate at every meal.

In all fairness to the Basic Four eating plan, it served its purpose: to virtually wipe out vitamin-deficiency diseases (pellagra, beriberi, scurvy, and the like) in the United States. But the Basic Four has a few serious flaws and relying on it alone for nutritional guidance has given rise to a host of new diseases. We now know that the typical modern-day American diet is setting us on a collision course with cancer, heart disease, hypertension, stroke, diabetes, cirrhosis of the liver, obesity, and a long and depressing list of other diseases. Ignorance may have been bliss, but it has also been hazardous to our health.

It has taken a long time for the powers that be in America to publicize our suicidal eating patterns, largely because of pressure from the food industry, which profits from our consumption of their unhealthy wares. The first inroads were made in 1977 when Senator George McGovern's Senate Select Committee on Nutrition and Human Needs bucked the tide by establishing a new set of "Dietary Goals for the United States." The McGovern committee recommended a diet with less fat (particularly the artery-clogging saturated kind), cholesterol, refined sugar, salt, alcohol and calories, and more fiber and complex carbohydrates. If adopted by all Americans, the committee estimated, such changes would bring about dramatic results: 80 percent fewer obese Americans, a 25-percent reduction of heart-attack deaths, a 50-percent decrease in diabetes deaths and a 1-percent annual increase in life expectancy.

The guidelines came at an opportune time politically, and the Departments of Agriculture and Health, Education and Welfare latched onto the recommendations. Needless to say, the meat, dairy, egg and processed food industries weren't exactly overjoyed. In 1980, the two agencies published what was, in the face of our long-standing attitudes, a revolutionary document. *Nutrition And Your Health: Dietary Guidelines For Americans* is a pithy pamphlet outlining the principles established by the Senate Select Committee. Although the guidelines have done a great deal to change attitudes in the past few years, they are still unknown — or unheeded — by most Americans. And the guidelines are already in danger. The USDA, under an administration a bit more sympathetic to big business, is now attempting to carve the substance out of them.

Despite such efforts, however, evidence to support the validity of the guidelines continues to mount. The latest blow on the side of good health came from a 1982 report entitled *Diet, Nutrition, and Cancer,* released by a special committee of the National Academy of Sciences. Most prominent among its findings was the definite link between fat consumption and colon, breast and prostate cancers, which account for one-third of all cancers in this country and afflict 270,000 Americans each year.

The committee also expressed concern over the ingestion of nitrosamines and polycyclic aromatic hydrocarbons, substances used in salt-cured, salt-pickled and smoked foods. Although most members did not deem evidence sufficient enough to make specific recommendations, they acknowledged evidence that high-protein diets are linked to increased risk of certain cancers. The committee also recommended things we *should* eat. Vegetables and fruits high in vitamin C and beta-carotene (the precursor to vitamin A), may deter cancer, along with foods rich in dietary fiber and the mineral selenium. The committee stressed the importance of deriving these nutrients from foods — not from vitamin supplements — to reduce the risk of cancer.

The NAS report recommended specifically that we:

• Reduce our consumption of fats, both saturated and unsaturated, to 30 percent of caloric intake.

• Eat fruits, vegetables and whole-grain products every day, especially those high in vitamin C and beta-carotene, like citrus fruits and dark green and yellow vegetables.

• Reduce our consumption of salt-cured, salt-pickled and smoked foods like smoked sausages, smoked fish, bacon, bologna and hot dogs.

• Drink alcohol in moderation, particularly if we also smoke.

Discussing the recommendations, committee chairman Dr. Clifford Grobstein said, "It is time to spread further the message that cancer is not as inevitable as death and taxes. Appropriate personal decision and public health measures can reduce cancer risk and the social cost and human tragedy it entails."

The new "producer-farmer-oriented" USDA is now attempting to downplay these findings. Nevertheless, what many have suspected for some time has now received official endorsement from some government agencies, which are traditionally the last to know — or at least the last to admit to — such findings. The message is clear: unless we want to continue our path toward ill health and premature death, we've got to make some changes in our diets. For you as prospective parents, the timing of these revelations is most propitious. Not only are you young enough that altering your diet will improve your own chances of avoiding disease, but you can start your youngster off on the right foot as soon as — and before — he's born. With your help and your example, he can begin at birth to form healthy habits for the rest of his life.

TAILORING YOUR DIET TO THE NEW NUTRITION

Perhaps it's our history. Americans seem to have a penchant for revolution, even on a small scale. As our divorce rate indicates, we prefer to end a relationship rather than save one. When it comes to losing weight, we'd rather commit ourselves to some torturous — and usually futile — regimen for a few months than make the most minor changes to our daily diet and exercise pattern, even if the latter is the only thing that guarantees permanent results. If told they could improve their chances of avoiding cancer, heart attack and other major killers by adopting some bizarre plan for a designated period of time, most Americans would jump on the bandwagon. But tell them they

Sugar, salt, caffeine and foods high in fat contribute to high blood pressure, overweight and hypertension when consumed in excess.

can achieve that goal by making subtle, yet permanent, changes to their lifestyles and they're likely to balk. It's not interesting, not flashy, not revolutionary enough. If feeling good, looking good, enjoying good health and providing a good example for your youngster are important to you, consider this simple and relatively painless plan.

Cut Down On Fats

There is no more doubt: The blackest mark against the American diet is its high fat and cholesterol content. Typically, Americans get more than 40 percent of their daily calories from fat. . .and it is hurting us. Compared to the Japanese, American men are six times as likely to die of a heart attack. The Japanese get only about 15 percent of their calories from fat. It used to be 10 percent, until Western influence in eating habits changed that. Similarly, breast and colon cancers are five times as common in the United States. The goal for optimum health is to get fat consumption as low as possible — at least at or, better yet, below the 30-percent mark recommended by the NAS committee. It's surprising the ways you can cut fat and cholesterol from your diet with a minimum of effort and sacrifice. Following are some examples.

• Eat less meat. Cut down on the size of meat servings and eat it less often. Contrary to what you've always been told (usually by the meat industry), you don't have to — and shouldn't — eat meat at every meal, or even every day. Cut meat out little by little, to the point where you're eating it only a few times a week. If you decide to cut it out altogether, all the better. Use meat as a condiment rather than as the focus of the meal.

• Buy lesser grades of meat ("good" instead of "choice"). They are not of lesser quality; they have less fat marbling, a lower fat content and fewer calories.

• Remove as much fat as possible from the meat you do serve. By doing so, it's possible to cut the fat and calorie content of some meats by more than half. For example, an eight-ounce T-bone steak with all the fat attached has about 700 calories, 83 percent come from fat. The same steak, trimmed, has 185 calories, 42 percent from fat.

• Although admirable sources of vitamins and minerals, organ meats like liver are very high in fat and cholesterol. Eat them in moderation.

• Cut down your intake of weiners (more than 75 percent of calories from fat), luncheon meats, bacon, sausage and canned and other high-fat meats.

• Use lean ground beef (190 calories per three-ounce patty, 47 percent from fat), not the regular variety (240 calories, 63 percent of them from fat). Drain ground meat on paper before serving.

• To make poultry a low-fat food, remove skin before cooking.

• Instead of frying, roast, bake, broil, barbecue or simmer meat, poultry and fish without added fat. Bake or broil meat on a rack, which allows fat to drain away.

• Not all fish is low-fat. Eat salmon, mackerel, herring, sardines, and trout — all of which contain more fat — in moderation. Buy tuna packed in water, not oil, and avoid fried fish.

• Reduce consumption of eggs, which are high in cholesterol. When preparing scrambled eggs or omelets, use one whole egg and one egg white in place of two eggs. In baking, use two egg whites in place of one whole egg. Remember that fertilized eggs touted by health food enthusiasts have no more nutrients than regular eggs — and just as much fat and cholesterol.

• When you make soups containing meat or poultry, make them ahead and refrigerate. Skim the congealed fat off the top before heating and serving.

• Read labels of frozen and processed foods carefully to determine if fats are major ingredients.

• Use vegetable oil in place of lard or shortening and a non-hydrogenated margarine in place of butter (choose a margarine whose first ingredient is a liquid polyunsaturated oil). Even after you've made the switch, use less oil and margarine in cooking and at the table. Avoid coconut and palm oils, which are higher in saturated fat than animal fats and are common ingredients in processed and "health" foods.

• Switch to non-fat — at the very least, low-fat — dairy products, including non-fat milk, buttermilk, low-fat yogurt and cottage cheese. A cup of whole milk contains 160 calories, half of them from fat; a cup of non-fat milk has only 90 calories, 2 percent of them from fat.

• Reduce consumption of cheese; whenever possible, purchase low-fat or skim-milk cheeses.

• Avoid sauces, gravies and creamed soups made with fat, butter, eggs, whole milk or cream.

• The following foods are also high in fat and should be eaten in moderation: coconuts, avocados, pork, nuts, seeds and peanut butter.

• Reduce or eliminate consumption of snack foods such as potato and corn chips (just 10 potato chips have 110 calories, 64 percent of them fat), and commercial sweets (pies, cakes, cookies, ice cream, etc.).

• Go easy on salad dressings (almost all fat and an astronomical 75 to 100 calories per tablespoon), mayonnaise, tartar sauce, and other high-fat condiments. Purchase reduced-calorie (less oil) commercial salad dressings, or flavor salad with lemon, vinegar and herbs. Consult the recipe books listed at the end of this chapter for some low-fat dressing ideas.

• Recognize fat in food easily with *The Fat Counter Guide* by Ronald M. Deutsch (Palo Alto, CA: Bull Publishing) or the handy new poster, "Lifesaver Fat & Calorie Guide" put out by the Center For Science In The Public Interest. Other anti-fat aids appear in the reading list at the end of this book.

Reduce Sodium Intake

Although the United States is number one in incidences of some diseases, the Japanese have more hypertension. It affects 40 percent of the country's population and is the leading cause of death and disability. Although the average American consumes far more sodium (four to eight grams per day, equal to 10 to 20 grams of table salt or two to four teaspoons) than is considered adequate and safe (one to three grams), the average Japanese person consumes even more. In cultures where almost no salt is consumed, hypertension is virtually nonexistent. Cutting down on salt is vital to the 20 percent of Americans who suffer from hypertension (making them susceptible to stroke, cardiovascular disease and kidney failure), but it is also important to the average American. Excess sodium also contributes to other problems, including water retention and more severe premenstrual symptoms. The McGovern committee recommended restricting salt intake to five grams per day (equal to two grams or 2000 mg of sodium), but you would do well to consume even less, particularly if you are genetically prone to hypertension.

Once you get used to less salt in your food — and it won't take long — you'll discover just how good foods really taste, and you'll probably lose your taste for salty processed and restaurant foods altogether. Here's how to begin:

• You can start slowly by using less salt at the table and then eliminating it completely.

• Reduce the salt called for in recipes and gradually eliminate most or all of it, too. Experiment with herbs and spices, wine, garlic, onions, lemon, lime and vinegar to flavor foods instead. There are a number of low-sodium cookbooks listed at the end of this chapter, but you can modify your own recipes too. Leave salt out of baked goods, and use low-sodium baking powder (available in health-food stores) and low-sodium baking soda (potassium bicarbonate). Consult your doctor, however, about the use of salt substitutes; for some people, they provide potentially dangerous levels of potassium.

• Two-thirds of the salt we eat comes from processed foods. Fresh, whole foods carry varying degrees of sodium, but insignificant amounts compared to processed foods. Nothing touched by human hands — from soft drinks to soup — is free of salt. The worst offenders are bacon, cold cuts, dried beef, hot dogs, corned beef, pastrami, liverwurst, sausage, meats (canned, kosher, pickled and smoked), poultry and fish, commercial sauces and condiments (barbecue sauce, tartar sauce, ketchup, mustard, Worcestershire sauce, and soy sauce), baked goods, bread, breakfast cereals, butter, bouillon cubes, commercial mixes of all kinds (cake, pudding, hot chocolate, pizza, meat "helpers"), commercial sauces and gravies, salad dressings, frozen dinners and other convenience foods, soft drinks, meat tenderizers (and other MSG-containing products), olives, dips, canned foods of all kinds, pickles, potato chips and other snack foods, salted crackers and nuts, sauerkraut, and finally all fast foods and most foods served in traditional restaurants.

• Low-sodium foods appear on the market every day and some of them can be very useful. Low-sodium tomato products (sauce, whole tomatoes and paste) allow you to cook low-salt dishes without spending hours in the kitchen making tomato sauce from scratch. I also recommend low-sodium cheese, butter and margarine, crackers, pretzels and nuts. When it comes to soups and entrees, however, I suggest that you make your own. Most commercial, saltless products of this type are terrible. The manufacturers have removed the salt, but made no effort to season the product in other ways, which is perhaps an effort to dismiss the entire low-sodium trend by saying, "Well, we tried making salt-free foods, but nobody would buy them." Some canned vegetables without salt are also available, but they cost more and have fewer nutrients than the best no-salt variety: fresh. Because they are made for a small segment of the population — those on salt-restricted diets — most salt-free foods currently cost more (sometimes twice as much) as their salty counterparts. As public demand increases, however, saltless foods will come down in price.

• Check with your local water department about the sodium level of your tap water. If it's higher than 45 parts per million, drink bottled water or purchase a filter. Do not drink soft water, which is very high in sodium.

• Limit the number of meals you eat in restaurants — particularly fast-food establishments — and when you do dine out, ask that salt be omitted from those dishes prepared on the spot.

• Many over-the-counter drugs (antacids, cough syrups, and the like) are very high in sodium. Not all ingredients are listed on the labels, so check with your doctor if in doubt.

• Read food labels carefully, looking for disguised sources of sodium: salt, sodium, baking powder, baking soda (bicarbonate of soda), monosodium glutamate (MSG), sodium nitrate, sodium benzoate, and disodium phosphate.

• Get a book like *Salt: The Brand Name Guide to Sodium Content* by Michael Jacobson, Bonnie Liebman and Greg Moyer (Washington, D.C.: CSPI), or *The Barbara Kraus Sodium Guide To Brand Names & Basic Foods* (New York: Signet), which lists the sodium contents of thousands of common foods, or *Sodium Content of Foods,* a pamphlet available from the Office of

Governmental and Public Affairs, Room 507A. USDA, Washington, DC 20250.

Sugar In Moderation

The word on sugar isn't sweet: The average American eats about 130 pounds of the stuff a year, which contributes to tooth decay, obesity, diabetes and hypoglycemia. Sugar adds nothing to the diet but a lot of empty calories, contributing to the staggering statistic that the average American weighs four pounds more than he did in 1962. It has been recommended that sugar intake be reduced from today's average of 18 percent of calories to 10 percent or less. On a 2000-calorie diet, that averages out to about 12 teaspoons of sugar a day. That may sound like a lot — and it is — but remember that you can get as many as nine teaspoons in a single 12-ounce soft drink.

• Reduce or eliminate consumption of the obviously sugar-laden stuff like cakes, cookies, candy and sugared cereals. Remember, too, that practically all processed foods are hiding places for sugar, so steer clear of them. Look for sugar on the label under these pseudonyms: sucrose, dextrose, fructose, glucose and other words ending in "ose," honey, molasses, brown sugar, raw sugar, maple, corn and other syrups, and sugar alcohols such as sorbitol, mannitol, maltitol, and xylitol. Remember, sugar is sugar, no matter what form it takes.

• Don't keep a sugar bowl on your table; it encourages everyone to use it. Cut down first and then try to eliminate sugar in coffee and tea, and use fresh fruit and raisins to sweeten cereal.

• Don't buy sweets and don't keep them in the house.

• For dessert, serve fresh fruit. The natural sugar in fruit is accompanied by a big batch of vitamins, minerals and fiber. Dried fruits, which have a very high sugar concentration, should be eaten in moderation; they also stick to the teeth and cause decay, so should always be followed by toothbrushing.

• For occasional treats, bake your own "sweets." Cut way down on the sweetener called for or substitute dried fruit or fruit juice, which at least offer other nutrients.

• Fresh fruit is preferable to fruit juice for breakfast and snacks because it retains the natural fiber and is more filling.

• If you buy canned fruits, buy those packed in their own juice rather than syrup.

• Serve wholesome snacks — fruit, raw vegetables, popcorn, cheese and crackers, nuts — instead of sweets.

• Don't substitute saccharin for sugar or buy "dietetic" foods and beverages that contain it. Saccharin has its own set of dangers and does nothing to rid you of that craving for a sweet taste.

• Never reward your child with sweets or use them as an incentive for finishing meals.

• Finally, and perhaps most important, as nutrition writer Jane Brody suggests, *"Eliminate soft drinks from your diet.* This one measure could bring about half the reduction in sugar consumption that was recommended in the Dietary Goals."

And Take These Steps, Too

• Cut down on animal protein. Protein, aside from its many other functions, is needed by the body to build and maintain body tissues, but most Americans get an estimated two to three times more than they need. Protein is not used for fuel (unless the body is totally depleted of fats and carbohydrates), and it burns inefficiently, leaving nitrogen behind that the liver and kidneys must work overtime to get rid of. Thus, excessive consumption of protein can sometimes cause dehydration, diarrhea and loss of appetite. Too much of the good thing can also interfere with proper absorption of calcium, which is already in short supply in the average diet. There are also indications that high-protein diets *may* be linked to certain cancers. But probably the main concern about high-protein foods is that they are generally high in fat, too.

• Increase consumption of complex carbohydrates and fiber. Cut back on the simple carbohydrates or sugars, substituting instead complex carbohydrates or starches, found primarily in vegetables, legumes and whole grains. The American public has been misinformed about carbohydrates for a long time. The belief, for example, that they are fattening is just one of the food myths that keeps Americans on an unhealthy diet. In reality, carbohydrates are the best source of energy. They're low in calories (carbohydrates and protein each have four calories per gram, while fat has nine) but high in vitamins and minerals (protein, too), inexpensive, and they contain healthy quantities of fiber, which aids in elimination and guards against constipation, diverticular disease, hemorrhoids, varicose veins, high serum cholesterol and obesity. They also might help prevent cancer. It is suggested that you get at least 55 percent of your daily calories from carbohydrates (and 15 percent from protein and 30 percent from fat), but if you can increase the amount of carbohydrates even more (at the expense of fats), all the better. To do so, eat a diet rich in a wide variety of fresh fruits and vegetables. Eat vegetables raw whenever possible, or steam them lightly to maintain nutrients. Eat dried beans and peas in place of meat. Buy whole-grain products whenever possible, including brown rice, whole wheat pasta, whole-grain breads, cereals, crackers and tortillas. Use whole-grain flour in your own cooking; it has more vitamins and fiber than white, enriched flour.

• Eat a wide variety of foods every day to make sure you get all the nutrients you need. If you eat the same foods every day, you could be shortchanging yourself on certain nutrients. Remember that the "Basic Four" is still a good guide, as long as you trim the fat out of it. A modified version of the program would look like this:

Vegetable/Fruit Group — Four servings per day (in addition to those substituted for animal foods). Eat a wide variety, including one serving each high in vitamin C and beta-carotene.

Bread/Cereal Group — Four servings per day (in addition to those substituted for animal foods). Buy whole-grain varieties of bread, cereal, crackers, flour, pasta and rice.

Protein (formerly the "Meat") Group — Two servings per day. Eat plenty of beans, peas, lentils, soybeans, whole-grains, vegetables, nuts, seeds, peanut butter, fish, and poultry with skin removed. Cut down on meat and eggs.

Milk Group — Adults: Two servings per day; teen-agers: four servings per day; Children: three servings per day. Use non-fat and low-fat milk, buttermilk, cheese, cottage cheese, ice milk and yogurt. Avoid cream, ice cream, sour cream, cream cheese and whole-milk products.

Vegetables and fruits are good for your growing baby. Babies especially love bananas; they're naturally sweet, nutritious and easy to eat.

Many low-sugar cereals are sold at the supermarket. As the saying goes, bread is the staff of life. Try to eat whole grain products.

Protein is important for your baby. Foods high in protein and low in fat include fish, poultry, peanut butter and tofu, which is made of soybeans. Peanut butter is high in fat, but it's unsaturated.

Although some children are allergic to them, milk products are an ideal source of nutrition for most infants. Look for the non- or low-fat varieties.

• Reduce overall calorie consumption and maintain your ideal weight. Obesity (40 percent of Americans are overweight by 10 or 20 pounds or more), is one of our greatest health problems, a known contributor to many diseases, including hypertension and diabetes. What's more, if you are overweight, chances are your child will be, too. Remember, also, that taking weight off and keeping it off is virtually impossible without exercise, which has the added benefit of being an all-around contributor to good health. For more about the vital role of exercise in weight loss, I recommend the following books: *The 200 Calorie Solution* by Dr. Martin Katahn (W.W. Norton); *California Diet And Exercise Program* by Dr. Peter Wood (Anderson World); *The Dieter's Dilemma* by Dr. William Bennett and Joel Gurin (Basic Books).

• Reduce consumption of harmful chemicals, including caffeine, alcohol (which is high in calories), nicotine, saccharin and other food additives.

• Drink more water. It's essential for proper bodily functions, aids digestion and elimination, and is filling and free of calories.

So that's it — the "new nutrition" in a nutshell. Sound like a tall order? It's not if you make changes gradually. When you assess the situation, the sacrifices are few and the rewards great. Start today and good nutrition will be second nature by the time your child is born.

SMART SUBSTITUTIONS

For	Substitute
Whole milk	Non-fat or low-fat milk or buttermilk
Butter	Margarine
Sour cream	Yogurt or buttermilk
Cream	Evaporated milk
Ice cream	Ice milk or frozen yogurt
2 eggs	1 whole egg and 1 egg white

Cheese	Skim-milk or low-fat cheese
Salt	Herbs, spices, black or red pepper, lemon juice
Soy sauce	Beer or wine
White bread, rolls and biscuits	Whole-grain bread, sourdough or pita bread
Rich sauces	Lemon juice, yogurt, margarine, herbs
Salad dressing	Lemon juice, herbs, onions or chives, wine vinegar, commercial or homemade reduced-oil dressings, garlic, seasoned tomato juice
Cakes and cookies	Sponge cake, angelfood cake, fruit, homemade breads or muffins
Potato chips	Unsalted pretzels or low-fat crackers like Rye Krisp
Peanuts	Popcorn, plain and with a minimum of salt
Canned fruit with syrup	Fresh fruit, fruit packed in water or own juice
Tuna packed in oil	Tuna packed in water
Cold cuts	Sliced turkey or chicken
French fries	Baked or boiled potato with lemon and pepper, buttermilk, or yogurt and chives
Sugar or saccharin-sweetened soft drinks	Mineral water or seltzer with lemon or lime wedge, apple or other fruit juice mixed with seltzer, tangy fresh-squeezed lemonade, iced herb or regular tea

COOKING UP GOOD HEALTH

Most of us have favorite foods and recipes; cooking healthy meals for your family doesn't necessarily mean leaving them all by the wayside. You can do your recipes a world of good by changing cooking techniques and reducing or eliminating ingredients like sugar and salt, or by making substitutions like those outlined in the chart in this chapter. But if you would like to try out some new, nutritious dishes or would find it easier to have low-fat, low-sodium, high-fiber recipes all laid out for you, visit your local bookstore or library and give one or more of the following cookbooks a try. They'll prove how easy and delicious healthy dining can be. If you go out cookbook browsing on your own, a few tips are in order:

• Beware of cookbooks (like the *Weight Watchers* series) that rely heavily on artificial sweeteners like saccharin.

• All vegetarian cookbooks are not necessarily low-sodium, low-fat cookbooks. Many call for sea salt (identical to ordinary salt in sodium content), soy sauce, miso and other salty ingredients. Often, too, they rely heavily on eggs, cheese, whole milk, coconut, nuts, avocado and other fatty foods. Peruse ingredient lists.

• It's difficult to find a perfect cookbook; most have one ax to grind (low-sodium, for example) and ignore all other aspects of good nutrition. Adjust recipes accordingly.

• Be realistic. Sure, you can be the consummate good foods cook by baking your own bread and making your own yogurt. But will you? The reason convenience foods have taken such a hold in our culture is that we are all so busy. It takes a lot of time to make your own pasta from wheat you grind at home. If you don't have the time or inclination to do so, pass up the hard-core health food cookbooks. Instead, purchase one that allows you to serve up healthy meals without having to spend 16 hours a day in the kitchen. The following are examples of some good cookbooks full of wholesome, easy recipes both you and your child will like:

Craig Claiborne, *Craig Claiborne's Gourmet Diet*.

Pamela Westland, *The High-Fiber Cookbook*.

Iva Bennett and Martin Simon, *The Prudent Diet*.

C.B.Y. Bond, et al, *The Low-Fat, Low Cholesterol Diet*.

M. Cavaiani, *The Low Cholesterol Cookbook*.

Carol Cutler, Haute Cuisine For Your Heart's Delight.

Ruthe Eshleman and Mary Winston, *The American Heart Association Cookbook*.

Nathalie Havenstein, *The Anti-Coronary Cookbook*.

Kay Heiss, *Eat to Your Heart's Content*.

Sylvia Rosenthal, *Live High on Low Fat*.

Polly Zane, *The Jack Sprat Cookbook*.

Low Fat and Vegetable Oil Recipes, Cleveland Clinic Research Division, 2020 E. 43rd St., Cleveland, OH.

Jeanne Jones, *The Calculating Cook*.

Jeanne Jones, *Diet For A Happy Heart*.

Jeanne Jones, *Secrets of Salt-Free Cooking*.

The Family Cookbook, The American Dietetic Association, 430 N. Michigan Ave., Chicago.

Betty Crocker's New American Cooking.

Jon N. Leonard and Elaine A. Taylor, *The Live Longer Now Cookbook*.

Frances Moore Lappe, *Diet For A Small Planet,* second edition.

Ellen Buchman Ewald, *Recipes For A Small Planet*.

Laurel Robertson, et al., *Laurel's Kitchen*.

Nikki and David Goldbeck's American Wholefoods Cuisine.

Joyce Daly Margie and James C. Hunt, *Living With High Blood Pressure: The Hypertension Diet Cookbook*.

Ellen Stern and Jonathan Michaels, *The Good Heart Diet Cookbook*.

Elma W. Bagg, *Cooking Without A Grain of Salt*.

Alma Payne and Dorothy Callahan, *The Fat & Sodium Control Cookbook*.

Francine Prince, *The Dieter's Gourmet Cookbook*.

Francine Prince, *The Best of Francine Prince's Diet Gourmet Recipes*.

Joyce Daly Margie, Robert I. Levy, James C. Hunt, *Living Better — Recipes For A Healthy Heart*.

Nutrition 1985 Cookbook, Nutrition 1985, Whitworth College, Spokane, WA 99251.

EATING RIGHT DURING PREGNANCY

You're about to bring a new life into the world. Your decision was probably not arrived at lightly. The world is a scary place and you won't be able to protect your child from all the harmful things in it. But it's nice to know that you can increase your child's chances for lifelong physical and mental health by watching your diet during your pregnancy.

If, in the past, you rationalized your own poor eating habits by saying, "I'm not hurting anybody but me," it's time to rethink your philosophy. First, *you* are important enough to eat correctly for all the time, not just when pregnancy makes special demands on your body. Secondly, you are now, as the well-worn cliche goes, eating for two. Your dining companion is a tiny human being who must be built from scratch. You are the sole supplier of the necessary tools and materials. Your unborn child is, literally, what you eat. Your diet now may have a greater effect on your child than anything he eats later in life.

If you've already begun to adopt the nutritional guidelines outlined in the last chapter, you're well on your way to a better life for yourself and a healthy pregnancy. The basics are all there; there's no need to alter the program except to increase your calorie intake somewhat and add extra amounts of certain vital nutrients.

WEIGHT GAIN

If you've been planning your pregnancy — or even if you haven't — ideally you should begin this nine-month adventure at your appropriate weight. If you're not at your ideal weight, this is certainly no time to start a diet that could rob you and your baby of necessary nutrients. Dieting can also lead to an excess of ketone bodies, by-products of fat breakdown, which can have a harmful effect on the fetus. An estimated 80,000 calories are needed to build a baby — that works out to an additional 300 a day that you, the mother, must consume. If you are active or underweight at conception, you may need more.

For a time, "skinny" pregnancies were in vogue, partly because toxemia, a complication of late pregnancy marked by hypertension, proteinuria (the presence of protein in the urine) and edema (swelling) was mistakenly believed to be linked to too much weight gain. Doctors chastised their patients who gained more than 10 or 15 pounds. Subsequent study has revealed that such drastic weight control can lead to babies of lower than normal birth weight who are subject to complications in infancy. Optimal weight gain is now considered to be between 24 and 27 pounds. The baby of an underweight mother will do better if she gains more (approximately 30 pounds), while the offspring of an overweight mother will do better if she gains less (between 15 and 16 pounds). You should discuss with your doctor the desirable weight gain for you.

Although a certain amount of weight gain is now known to be desirable and necessary during pregnancy, the sky isn't the limit. In the same study that produced the foregoing figures, Dr. Richard L. Naeye of the department of pathology of the Hershey Medical Center at Pennsylvania State University College of Medicine found that infant mortality rates increase when mothers gain more than 32 pounds, regardless of their weight prior to pregnancy.

Your overall weight is important, but so is the rate at which you gain. Don't assume that if you put on too much weight at the outset, you can taper near the end of term. Most of the early weight gain is blood volume expansion, growth of the uterus and breasts and storage of fat, while most of the weight gained in the last few months is the baby's rapid growth. That's certainly not the time to cut your calories drastically. A sensible diet should allow you the desired pattern of weight gain: about two to four pounds the first three months and three to four pounds each month thereafter. That weight gain is accounted for as follows:

Baby	7.5 pounds
Placenta	1.5 pounds
Uterus	2.0 pounds
Increased blood and fluids	8.5 pounds
Bodily changes for breast-feeding	4.5 pounds

Much of the weight will be lost at delivery, of course, and even more during lactation. Continuation of a sensible eating plan should guarantee your return to pre-pregnancy weight within a reasonable time. Your weight gain during pregnancy should be slow and steady. If it jumps rapidly, consult your doctor.

DESIRABLE WEIGHTS BEFORE PREGNANCY

Height (feet-inches)	Weight (pounds) (Medium frame)
4-10	109-121
4-11	111-123
5	113-126
5-1	115-129
5-2	118-132
5-3	121-135
5-4	124-138
5-5	127-141
5-6	130-144
5-7	133-147
5-8	136-150
5-9	139-153
5-10	142-156
5-11	145-159
6	148-162

Courtesy of Metropolitan Life Insurance Co.
*In light clothing, based on height in one-inch heels.

Note: These figures were, much to the chagrin of many nutritionists and health professionals, recently revised upward.

WHAT YOU NEED

It's easy to put on weight, and it's easy to take in more calories. Making those calories pay for themselves in top-notch nutrition is another story. Your body will need more of just about everything while junior is growing, but some nutrients will be in greater demand. A little extra attention to diet should maintain an adequate supply.

Protein

Protein is the stuff of which muscles and tissues are made. More protein is needed during pregnancy to build reproductive tissue (the uterus and placenta) and provide the raw materials for your baby's body and brain cells. Inadequate protein can set the stage for retarded growth or mental deficiency.

During pregnancy, a woman's RDA for protein nearly doubles, jumping from 44 to 74 grams. Some nutritionists recommend 100 grams in the last months of pregnancy when fetal growth and brain cell development are accelerated. Getting all that protein in just 300 additional calories a day may sound tricky, but because many of us get nearly twice what we need on a daily basis, it shouldn't be a problem. Protein is so crucial to your baby's health that all women, particularly women in a low income bracket who may not be able to afford protein items, who constantly watch their weight, or whose busy lifestyles cause them to eat sporadically or poorly, should evaluate their diets to be sure they are getting enough. As a final incentive, it's now thought that toxemia (once linked to excess weight gain or too much sodium) is linked to protein deficiency.

You get nearly half the protein you need from the quart of non-fat milk you should consume everyday (see "Calcium"), but it's also recommended that you eat approximately four servings of other protein-rich foods. We tend to think of protein in terms of meat, fish, poultry, cheese and other dairy products, but don't forget the high-quality, low-fat protein contained in dried beans and peas, whole grains and vegetables, especially if they're combined.

A small amount of meat, fish, poultry or cheese can also increase the protein quality of a largely vegetarian meal. (Besides lowering your intake of saturated fat, limiting animal protein in your diet can also reduce your ingestion of chemical residues in animal fat that can reach your baby through the placenta). Nuts and seeds are also excellent protein sources, but too high in fat (even though unsaturated) and calories to eat in anything but moderate quantities.

Remember, you need about four servings of protein a day. Serving sizes can be determined from the following list. Significant amounts of protein are also found in whole grains (wheat, oats, rye, buckwheat, brown rice, wheat germ, corn meal, barley, and whole-grain breads, cereals and pastas) and vegetables (spinach, broccoli, bean sprouts, artichokes, cauliflower, brussels sprouts, mushrooms, peas, potatoes, sweet potatoes and corn), particularly when eaten in certain combinations. For example: pizza, beans with tortillas, and vegetables with brown rice are all excellent sources of protein.

Food

One Serving

Food	One Serving
Vegetable	varies
Whole grains	varies
Dried peas, lentils, dried or canned beans (kidney, garbanzo, black, navy, mung, pinto	1 cup
Soybeans	3/4 cup
Peanut and other nut butters	4 tablespoons
Nuts	1/2 cup
Seeds (sunflower, sesame, pumpkin)	1/2 cup
Tofu	1 cup
Cottage cheese	1/2 cup
Non-fat or low-fat milk	2 cups
Yogurt	2 cups
Natural cheese (cheddar, Swiss, Monterey jack)	2 ounces
Beef, pork, fish, shellfish, chicken, turkey, veal, organ meat (fat trimmed, skin removed)	2 to 3 ounces
Eggs	2

Calcium

Calcium is the main structural element of bones and teeth, so its dramatically increased need during pregnancy is not surprising. The mineral is also essential to other vital functions, including transmission of nerve impulses and muscle contractions. Most women have trouble getting enough calcium; pregnancy greatly compounds the problem. If you aren't getting adequate calcium, your baby may still get what he needs, but at your expense.

An estimated 25 percent of postmenopausal women suffer from osteoporosis (weakened bones that break easily) caused by chronic calcium shortage. Although calcium absorption increases during pregnancy and the amount is adequate for both mother and baby, a woman's calcium deficiency later in life may begin at this time. There are others, however, who believe that more damage is done in the years after pregnancy when an inadequate supply of calcium causes it to be pulled from the bones in order to maintain a constant level in the blood and meet the need for calcium elsewhere in the body.

Although it's difficult to get the 800 mg of calcium usually recommended for women (some experts feel the RDA is inadequate and should be set at 1000 mg for women before menopause and 1200 to 1500 after), it's even more of a challenge to get the 1200 recommended during pregnancy unless you diligently consume milk products. To avoid fat, drink a quart of non-fat milk a day. It supplies more than 1400 mg. Some of that milk can be in the form of other low- or non-fat dairy products like yogurt, ice milk, skim cheeses and buttermilk.

You can also fulfill your calcium quota by eating puddings, soups, sauces, baked goods, cereals and other dishes containing milk. Or try adding non-fat dry milk to baked goods, meat loaf and blender drinks. The calcium in dairy products is more readily absorbed, but you can also derive significant amounts from many vegetables, especially greens like spinach and broccoli.

Getting enough calcium is one thing, absorbing it is quite another. Vitamin D is needed to absorb calcium, yet most foods are poor sources of that vitamin. It's recommended that you buy milk fortified with vitamin D. On the other hand, absorption of calcium is hindered by too much protein, phosphorus or fat in the diet (although a moderate amount of fat aids absorption).

HIGH IN CALCIUM, LOW IN FAT

	Calcium (mg)
Low-fat milk, 1 cup	352
Non-fat milk, 1 cup	296
Cottage cheese (low-fat), 1 cup	131
Yogurt (low-fat), 1 cup	294
Ice-milk, 1 cup	204
Mozzarella cheese (part skim), 1 oz.	210
Ricotta cheese (from skim milk), ½ cup	330
Beet greens (boiled, drained), 1 cup	144
Spinach (boiled), 1 cup	167
Turnip greens (boiled), 1 cup	267
Tofu, 2x3x1-inch piece	150
Broccoli (boiled), medium-size stalk	158
Molasses (dark or blackstrap), 1 tbsp.	137
Okra (boiled, sliced), 1 cup	147

Your Goal: 1200 mg per day.

What a Quart of Non-fat Milk* Provides

		percentage needed during pregnancy	percentage needed during breast-feeding
Calories	353	15	14
Protein	35.3g	47	55
Vitamin A	400 mcg	40	33
Thiamine	0.34 mg	24	23
Riboflavin	1.76 mg	117	104
Niacin	0.7 mg	5	4
Vitamin C	10 mg	12	10
Vitamin D	10 mcg	100	100
Calcium	1186 mg	99	99
Phosphorus	931 mg	78	78
Iron	0.4 mg	less than 1 percent	less than 1 percent

*Fortified with vitamins A and D

Phosphorus is a problem for those who drink a lot of soft drinks (which contain phosphoric acid) and eat processed foods with phosphate additives.

Because of recent attention to the long-term effects of calcium deficiency in women, many experts now recommend calcium supplements. Consult your physician for his views. And don't forget exercise, one of the best defenses against bone deterioration.

Iron

Iron is required by the body in such minute quantity (18 mg normally, 30 to 60 mg during pregnancy) that it's difficult to fathom its crucial role in the formation of red blood cells. Small requirement or not, iron, like calcium, is something most women have difficulty getting enough of. Once again, the problem is magnified during pregnancy when a mother's blood volume doubles. Without an adequate intake of the mineral, supplying the fetus' needs can leave the mother anemic (with smaller-than-normal red blood cells incapable of transporting oxygen), a condition characterized by weakness, fatigue, headaches, pallor and a greater susceptibility to infection.

Few foods are ideal sources of iron, and the amount you absorb is nowhere near the amount you ingest. Most women probably need an iron supplement on a regular basis; during pregnancy it's absolutely essential. Your doctor will probably recommend a supplement of between 30 and 60 mg. In addition, you should try to eat as many iron-rich foods as possible. Cooking in iron pots also helps.

Liver is a good source of iron; there are about 7.5 mg of iron in three ounces of beef or chicken liver, and a whopping 12 mg in calf's liver. It may be high in cholesterol (372 mg in those same three ounces), but liver is so rich in iron and other vitamins and minerals that you should serve it every week or two. Menstruating, pregnant and lactating women should take special care to get plenty of iron.

Vitamin A

Liver is also a rich source of vitamin A, perfect to eat during pregnancy when the requirement increases from 800 to 1000 micrograms. Vitamin A is a fat-soluble vitamin that can be stored in the body; a single serving of liver provides a nine-day supply. In

High in Iron

Iron (mg)

Spinach, 1 cup
- raw 1.7
- cooked 4.0

Beets greens (cooked), 1 cup 2.8
Parsley, 1 tbsp. 0.2
Asparagus (cooked), 4 medium spears 0.4
Broccoli, medium stalk, steamed 1.4
Loose-leaf lettuce, 1 cup 0.8
Kidney beans (canned), 1 cup 4.6
Dried beans, 1 cup . . . . .12 to 14
Tomato paste, ½ cup 4.6
Lentils (cooked), 1 cup 4.2
Soybean flour (defatted), 1 cup 11.1
Wheat germ, 1 tbsp. 0.5
Whole-wheat flour, 1 cup 4.0
Brewer's yeast, 1 tbsp. 1.4
Shredded wheat, 1 biscuit 0.9
Tofu, 1 piece 2.3
Molasses, dark, 1 tbsp. 3.2
Dried apricots, 10 medium halves 1.9
Prunes, ½ cup 2.2
Prune juice, 6 oz. 7.9
Watermelon, 1 slice 2.1
Veal, 3 oz. 3.0
Beef liver (fried), 3 oz. 7.5
Chicken liver (chopped), ½ cup 6.0

addition to its many other tasks, vitamin A is necessary for the normal growth and repair of epithelial cells lining the respiratory, digestive and reproductive tracts and cells that form the outer layers of skin. Getting enough vitamin A is essential. Fortunately, that isn't difficult. In addition to liver, other organ meats are excellent sources of vitamin A in its preformed state. Whole or fortified milk and butter are other good choices. Nature has also provided a clever, non-fat way to get vitamin A. Many vegetables contain carotenes, precursors or provitamins that are readily converted to vitamin A in the body as needed. Many vitamin A-rich foods are easily recognized by the yellow-orange color lent them by the carotene pigments. But carotenes are also prevalent in many green plants. Get your vitamin A — at least one serving a day — the low-fat way in such foods as carrots and carrot juice, spinach, greens, parsley, cantaloupe, apricots, sweet potatoes, papaya, yellow squash, and a host of other fruits and vegetables.

Megadosing with vitamin A (including fish liver oils) is discouraged because of potential toxicity, but it is particularly hazardous during pregnancy. High doses have been linked to a variety of birth defects. Food — particularly plant foods which cannot cause toxicity or birth defects — is the safe, effective way to guarantee an ample supply.

B Vitamins

The B vitamins fulfill many essential roles, not the least is the conversion of food — including the extra food you consume during pregnancy — to energy. There is a greater need for all of the B's during pregnancy, particularly folacin, whose requirement is doubled from 400 to 800 mcg. Some women seem to have a greater-than-average need for folacin, and will require even more. Folacin is responsible for synthesizing an essential ingredient of DNA, without which cells do not divide and organisms do not grow.

A shortage of folacin most directly affects those cells — red and white blood cells and cells lining the intestinal tract — that have a rapid turnover rate. The main disease associated with folacin deficiency is macrocytic or megaloblastic anemia — characterized by large, undivided red blood cells. The human body is most susceptible to folacin deficiency in periods of growth when cell division — and DNA synthesis — takes place at an increased rate. Onset of deficiency symptoms is more rapid — and common — among pregnant and nursing women, infants and children. The hormonal changes of pregnancy also account for the increased need. As with B_6 and some other water-soluble vitamins, women taking oral contraceptives have lower levels of folacin in their blood. So if you were taking the pill prior to conception, you may have already been deficient.

Folacin was discovered in the 1930s during a search for the cause of megaloblastic anemia, which was common among pregnant women in India. That disease is still prevalent in developing nations. But even in the United States, a 1975 study of expectant mothers at an urban clinic showed that 16 percent had deficient red cell folate levels and another 14 percent had low levels. Increased need, more frequent urination and limited dietary intake make it difficult to get enough, particularly during pregnancy, without supplementation.

Some experts have recommended dietary supplements of 300 to 600 mcg of folacin during the last half of pregnancy. Your doctor may prescribe folacin for you or a daily multiple vitamin/mineral tablet that contains 100 percent of the folacin RDA for non-pregnant women, plus safe doses of the other vitamins, including the other Bs you may be getting in short supply.

Two other vitamins crucial to red blood cell formation are B_6 and B_{12}. Getting more of them during pregnancy is mandatory. Some women seem to have a greater-than-average need for vitamin B_6, so the recommended 2.6 mg for pregnancy may not be enough. Without an adequate supply, the fetus can suffer. The extra B_6, like the B_{12}, should be obtainable from foods with just a little extra attention to your diet. The exception for B_{12} is strict vegetarians who eat no meat, fish, eggs or dairy products. Because B_{12} is found only in foods of animal origin, those individuals definitely need B_{12} supplements.

A final word about B vitamins: Although whole grains are a rich source, many B's are lost in milling and only three are added back to enriched products. So make every effort to eat whole grains.

HIGH IN B VITAMINS

B_1 (Thiamine)

Whole grains
Enriched grains
Wheat germ
Brewer's yeast
Legumes
Soybeans
Nuts
Oatmeal
Pork
Oysters
Liver and organ meats

B_2 (Riboflavin)

Green, leafy vegetables
Yeast
Enriched foods
Milk products
Liver and organ meats
Meat
Eggs

Niacin

Whole grains
Enriched grains
(continued)

Niacin   (*continued*)

Green, leafy vegetables
Peanuts
Brewer's yeast
Fish
Poultry
Lean meat
Liver and organ meats

Folacin

Green, leafy vegetables
Legumes
Whole grains
Nuts
Yeast
Liver and organ meats

B₁₂

Animal foods only:
Liver
Meat
Fish
Poultry
Milk
Eggs

B₆ (Pyridoxine)

Whole grains
Legumes
Corn
Wheat germ
Meat
Liver and organ meats

Biotin

Legumes
Nuts
Dark green vegetables
Yeast
Eggs
Liver and organ meats

Pantothenic Acid

Vegetables
Fruit
Whole grains
Legumes
Wheat germ
Yeast
Milk products
Salmon
Liver and organ meats

Vitamin C

Vitamin C is a controversial vitamin that has been touted as the cure for just about anything that ails you. So popular is it among health food proponents that some take as much as 10,000 mg a day. Although the RDA for vitamin C for women is currently 60 mg (80 mg for pregnant women), some scientists feel that keeping tissues at the saturation level, an intake of approximately 120 mg a day, is a safer bet. Vitamin C is vital in forming and maintaining cell and blood vessel walls, so don't skimp, especially during pregnancy.

The amount of vitamin C found in a daily multiple vita-min/mineral pill certainly won't hurt you, but megadosing on C during pregnancy is not a wise idea; your child could develop a dependency. Even if you believe in extra vitamin C, which may indeed have its advantages, you should have no trouble getting more than an adequate amount from food. One cup of orange juice contains 124 mg, and the vitamin is also abundant in other citrus fruits, cantaloupe, strawberries, potatoes, green and red peppers, tomatoes, tomato juice, broccoli, cabbage, and many other fresh fruits and vegetables.

Vitamin D

Vitamin D is used by the body almost exclusively in the formation of bones and teeth, a big job when you're building a baby. Among other things, vitamin D aids in the absorption of both calcium and phosphorus and helps deposit these minerals in the bones to give them the strength they need to support the body. The calcium in all that extra milk you're drinking wouldn't do you any good without vitamin D, so your recommended in-take is doubled during pregnancy, from five mcg to 10. Fortu-nately, most milk is fortified with D, and that's the kind you should buy.

Vitamin D is also available in fatty fish (tuna, salmon, herring and shrimp are all rich in D), eggs, liver and butter. You should eat them in moderation because of their high fat content. One rich source of vitamin D contains no fat or calories and costs nothing: sunshine. The vitamin is formed when ultraviolet light reacts with a sterol in the skin. A daily walk gives you vitamin D and improves your fitness at the same time. If you're drinking your fortified milk, eating moderate amounts of other D-rich foods and getting outside regularly, there should be no reason for supplementation. Remember: Vitamin D is a fat-soluble vitamin toxic in megadoses.

Vitamin E

The role of vitamin E in the body is not well-understood, but one of its more clearly defined functions is as an anti-oxidant. Vitamin E reacts with oxidizing agents or free radicals capable of causing damage to other more fragile molecules and disables them. It plays a major role in protecting other oxygen-sensitive nutrients like vitamin A, polyunsaturated fatty acids (used to build cell membranes), other cell membrane constituents and some enzymes. It may also be required in minute amounts for the synthesis of heme, part of the hemoglobin molecule.

During pregnancy, the need for vitamin E increases from eight to 10 mg a day. Vitamin E is prevalent in foods, however — especially whole grains, vegetable oils and wheat germ — so it should be available in more than adequate amounts in any well-balanced diet.

Sodium

Salt is needed in greater quantity during pregnancy to help balance the increased fluid volume, but even if you have cut down on sodium in your regular diet, chances are you are still getting more than enough of this ubiquitous mineral. Sodium is abundant in processed, canned, packaged, restaurant and fast foods, and varying amounts also occur naturally in most foods. Pregnancy is not the time to cut back on sodium drastically. It's okay to salt your food lightly (with iodized salt to meet your increased iodine need, too) and retain salt in recipes. If you suffer from hypertension, consult your physician about appropriate sodium intake.

Other Minerals

While the need for all nutrients is greater during pregnancy, the Food and Nutrition Board also lists specific increases of phosphorus, magnesium, iodine and zinc. All can be readily obtained in a well-balanced diet like the one recommended here. While the zinc intake of many pregnant women seems to be lower than suggested, you can get an adequate supply by consuming milk, meat, fish and eggs.

Fluids

Drinking plenty of liquids is a good idea all the time to help use nutrients, carry waste out of the body and regulate body temperature, but they are even more important during pregnancy to maintain your increased fluid volume. You need about six eight-ounce servings of liquids a day. Water is your best bet; fruit and vegetable juices are also good, but go easy on coffee, tea and soft drinks. You can also include soups in the total.

Increased Nutritional Needs for Pregnancy and Breast-feeding*

Nutrient	Non-Pregnant	Pregnant	Breast-feeding
Calories	2000	+300=2300	+500=2500
Protein, g	44	+30=74	+20=64
Vitamin A, R.E.	800	+200=1000	+400=1200
Vitamin D, mcg	5	+5=10	+5=10
Vitamin E, mg	8	+2=10	+3=11
Vitamin C, mg	60	+20=80	+40=100
Thiamine, mg	1	+0.4=1.4	+0.5=1.5
Riboflavin, mg	1.2	+0.3=1.5	+0.5=1.7
Niacin, mg	13	+2=15	+5=18
Vitamin B_6, mg	2	+0.6=2.6	+0.5=2.5
Folacin, mg	400	+400=800	+100=500
Vitamin B_{12}, mcg	3	+1=4	+1=4
Calcium, mg	800	+400=1200	+400=1200
Phosphorus, mg	800	+400=1200	+400=1200
Magnesium, mg	300	+150=450	+150=450
Iron, mg	18	+30–60=48–78	+30–60=48–78
Zinc, mg	15	+5=20	+10=25
Iodine, mcg	150	+25=175	+50=200

*Source: Recommended Dietary Allowances, Food and Nutrition Board, National Research Council, 1980

THINGS TO AVOID

Snack Foods

A successful eating schedule for many women during pregnancy is three light meals and several snacks. Now, as always, however, try to avoid the empty calories of traditional snack foods like cake, cookies, pie, candy, soft drinks and potato chips. You have a few extra calories to spend during pregnancy, but it is more important than ever that you get nutrients with them. Junk foods can quickly eat up your total without providing any nutrition. Three or four cookies easily account for the extra 300 calories you need in a day, but they contribute nothing in the way of nutrition. An equally satisfying snack of an apple and one ounce of cheddar cheese carries 200 calories or less and packs a powerful nutritional punch.

Eating for Two the Low-fat Way

Fruits and Vegetables	4 or more servings	Select 1 rich in Vitamin A (yellow-orange or dark green, leafy); 1 rich in Vitamin C (citrus, cantaloupe, tomato, strawberries); eat wide variety	Raw, steamed lightly, baked. Choose fresh or frozen; avoid canned. Season lightly; use margarine in moderation. For sauces, use non-fat milk or yogurt in place of cream or sour cream.
Whole grains	4 or more servings	Bread, cereal (hot and cold), brown rice, wheat germ, macaroni and pasta, crackers, pancakes, rolls, tortillas, muffins	Buy only whole-grain products; use whole-grain flours for pancakes and home-baked goods. Bake with margarine instead of butter, vegetable oil in place of shortening. Use more egg whites, fewer yolks. Use non-fat milk. To sweeten, use fruit juice, fresh or dried fruit, molasses in place of sugar or honey.
Non-Fat and Low-Fat Dairy Products	4 servings	Non-fat milk, yogurt, low-fat cottage cheese, part-skim cheese, buttermilk, ice milk, non-fat dry milk	Drink plain, use in soups, puddings, blender drinks, casseroles, baked goods and sauces
Protein foods	3 or more servings	Vegetables, whole grains, dried peas and beans, seeds, nuts, nut butters, fish (lean varieties), poultry (skin removed), meat (all fat trimmed), eggs (use 1 yolk, 2 whites)	Serve vegetable protein in combinations. If intake is largely vegetable, eat more servings. Avoid frying animal foods; instead, bake, broil, stew or barbecue. Roast on rack so fat drains away.

Caffeine

On those days when building a baby leaves you feeling fatigued, you may be tempted to reach for a cup of coffee or a can of soda. Try to resist. As you know, caffeine is a stimulant that affects the central nervous system. For most of us, it's a harmless pick-me-up in moderate quantities, but for others, it can cause insomnia, nervousness, irritability, anxiety, disturbances to heart rate and rhythm and other problems. Caffeine also acts as a diuretic, causing you to lose water too quickly along with vital minerals.

Caffeine poses even greater problems for the expectant mother. Like most other drugs, caffeine crosses the placenta, through which the baby receives nourishment from its mother. Although the data on caffeine is inconclusive, many believe there is just cause for the pregnant woman to beware. Some studies indicate that caffeine may cause birth defects, spontaneous abortions, stillbirths and premature births. The FDA recommends that pregnant women either avoid caffeine (and other substances with drug-like effects that cross the placenta) or use it sparingly. To do that, you must realize how prevalent caffeine is in commonly consumed foods, drugs and beverages, including the colas and other soft drinks that are a staple of the American diet. The following list can help, but be aware that caffeine is found in other over-the-counter and prescription drugs besides those listed here. No drug should be taken without approval from your physician.

Caffeine Content of Common Foods, Beverages and Drugs

Coffee, 1 cup	75 to 155 mg
Instant coffee, 1 cup	66 mg
Decaffeinated coffee, 1 cup	2 to 5 mg
Black tea, 1 cup	28 to 44 mg
Instant tea, 1 cup	24 to 131 mg
Cocoa, 1 cup	5 mg
Cola, 12 oz.	32 to 65 mg
Milk chocolate, 1 oz.	6 mg
Sweet or dark chocolate, 1 oz.	20 mg
Baking chocolate, 1 oz.	35 mg
No-Doz	100 mg
Vivarin	200 mg
Anacin	32 mg
Cope	32 mg
Excedrin	64.8 mg
Vanquish	33 mg
Dristan	16.2 mg
Neo-Synephrine	15 mg
Triaminicin	30 mg

Alcohol

Overconsumption of alcohol can have tragic effects on adult lives, but is even more devastating to the unborn. Fetal alcohol syndrome (FAS), characterized by retarded growth, impaired motor development, abnormal structural and facial characteristics and mental retardation, is thought to afflict three to five of every 1000 babies born, making alcohol one of the leading causes of birth defects. While FAS has been clearly established as a complication of chronic alcoholism, the effects of moderate drinking during pregnancy are serious, too, albeit more subtle.

One of the things they don't tell you in those glamorous and sexy alcohol ads is that "social drinking" (consumption of four drinks a day) can cause mental and behavioral problems for the unborn child. And as few as two drinks a day have been associated with low birth weight and structural abnormalities. Such problems have been connected to one-time binge drinking as well as chronic social drinking. No safe level has yet been established for alcohol consumption during pregnancy, so it is strongly suggested that the expectant mother stop drinking or at the very least, limit consumption to one or two drinks a day. There is just too much evidence that a good time or two can lead to a bad time for your baby.

Aside from its potentially harmful effects on the fetus, alcohol consumed regularly can affect the mother's appetite, inhibiting absorption of some nutrients, and by adding empty calories more wisely spent on nutrient-rich foods. Drinking can also increase your chances for a fall or some other potentially harmful accident.

For a predinner cocktail, try something refreshing and nutritious like fruit juice on the rocks, tomato or vegetable juice over cracked ice with a shot of Tabasco and a stalk of celery, or mineral water with a wedge of lemon or lime. If a drink before dinner relaxes you and whets your appetite, consider having half a glass of wine with ice and club soda or mineral water. Much of the pleasure in drinking comes from its social aspects, so a prospective father can help bolster his wife's resolve by abstaining, too.

Vitamin Megadoses

One of the biggest "fitness" fads of the past decade has been vitamin megadosing, the ingestion of supplements in amounts exceeding the RDAs by 10 to 100 times. Although the effectiveness of megadoses in a few instances shows promise, in most cases there are no proven benefits and some very real hazards.

Your doctor may prescribe vitamin/mineral supplements for you (particularly of iron, folic acid and the other B vitamins). These are useful and should be taken regularly. Don't prescribe extra vitamins for yourself, thinking that if some is good, more must be better. Large doses of the fat-soluble vitamins A and D have been shown to cause birth defects in animals, and while the water-soluble vitamins (B and C) probably pose less of a threat to fetal development, some evidence suggests that megadoses can induce a vitamin dependency in the newborn.

One report states that as little as 400 mg of C a day in the diets of pregnant women can result in infants with rebound scurvy. While in the uterus, the metabolic system of the fetus adjusts to excessive amounts of vitamin C ingested by the mother by speeding up excretion. After birth, when the infant is consuming only normal amounts of C, the excretion mechanism continues to work overtime, carrying out even the C the child needs to maintain normal serum and tissue levels. The unfortunate result: infantile scurvy, a deficiency disease that by this time should be nonexistent.

As a final note, we know that many vitamins work by interaction with one another. Taking large doses of one can affect levels of others and throw off the body's delicate balance. The same is true of minerals. According to an FDA report, some "can cause adverse health effects if an individual takes as little as twice as much as is required to maintain good health." Among the toxic effects are fetal abnormalities.

Smoking

Despite the romantic messages in cigarette advertising, we should all be aware by now of the major role cigarette smoking plays in cancer, respiratory disorders and heart disease. Giving up smoking is one of the strongest, wisest steps anyone can take toward better health. And mounting evidence shows that the smoker hurts more than himself.

Numerous studies have shown, for example, that a mother's smoking can have a detrimental effect on the fetus, slowing its growth and increasing its chances of being born at less than normal birth weight. Small babies are more likely to suffer complications in infancy. One study showed that when pregnant women smoked two cigarettes in succession, fetal breathing movements were diminished. And mortality rates at birth increase directly with the amount of maternal smoking during pregnancy.

As with all aspects of child-rearing, however, the responsibility is not all the mother's. Other studies have shown that children of smokers visit the hospital more frequently for respiratory infections during their first year than children of non-smokers. According to a report by the Committee on Environmental Hazards of The American Academy of Pediatrics, "The incidence of pneumonia and bronchitis during the first year of life was associated with the smoking habits of *either* parent, being lowest when both parents were non-smokers, highest when both smoked, and intermediate when only one parent smoked." If that isn't reason enough for both mom and dad to stop smoking for good, consider: Children of smokers are more likely to take up smoking — and at an earlier age — than children of non-smokers.

Drugs

The placenta was once thought to be a protective barrier that deflected harmful substances away from the fetus the same way that famous "invisible shield" protected teeth from cavities in old toothpaste commercials. But now we know that most things ingested by the mother, including most drugs, cross the placenta and reach the fetus. Unfortunately, every now and then a drug like thalidomide is proven to cause birth defects, and many other drugs have been shown to be harmful in animals. Other drugs are suspected, and should be avoided.

Among the drugs that can affect your baby are the hormones found in birth control pills. The FDA advises that "you should stop taking the pill immediately and consult your doctor if you become pregnant while taking the pill — or if you think you *may* have become pregnant. If you have been taking the pill and discontinue it in the hope of becoming pregnant, you should wait at least three months before attempting to conceive. During this waiting period, use some other form of contraception. A child conceived immediately after you stop using the pill could have a high risk of birth defects."

A host of other drugs have been shown to cause physical deformities, behavioral abnormalities, and even addiction in the infant. To be avoided in particular are heroin, methadone, amphetamines, barbiturates and tranquilizers of all types. Problems have also been associated with anticonvulsants administered for epilepsy (a greater risk of cleft lip or palate), and the antibiotic tetracycline (permanent discoloration of the child's teeth). Even aspirin, according to the FDA, "may prolong labor or cause excessive bleeding before and after delivery." Drugs used in delivery can also affect the infant in myriad ways, from depressing his respiration to reducing his sucking reflex temporarily. To assure the best start for your newborn, you've probably already decided on a method of delivery as drug-free as possible.

To be safe, check with your doctor before taking any over-the-counter remedies, including aspirin and other analgesics, antacids, cold and allergy tablets, motion sickness remedies, diuretics, laxatives or diet pills. See your doctor the moment you suspect you are pregnant. If you are taking regular prescription medication, ask him if it is safe to continue. Be sure that any doctor who prescribes medication for you is aware that you are pregnant. Realize, too, that all drugs aren't harmful. If your well-being is at stake, by all means take the medication prescribed for you. Leave the recreational drugs (including marijuana and cocaine) to others who have only their own health to worry about.

Food Additives

Chemicals added to foods to preserve color, flavor and texture have also been inadequately tested, especially with regard to their ability to cause birth defects. Saccharin and nitrites are believed to be carcinogenic and are probably best avoided, especially during pregnancy. That means no diet sodas, and go easy on cured meats like hot dogs, bacon and cold cuts, which are generally too high in fat and salt to eat often anyway. Avoid BHA, BHT, artificial colors and artificial flavors.

SPECIAL PROBLEMS OF PREGNANCY

Morning Sickness

Morning sickness afflicts roughly half of all pregnant women. Despite the name, the nausea and vomiting associated with this problem can strike at any time of day, generally during the first three months of pregnancy. Causes include hormonal changes, drops in blood sugar or slowed digestion. It's best to avoid antacids and cope with morning sickness in other ways.

If your case goes by the rules and sends you sailing to the bath-room at dawn's early light, keep the tried-and-true soda crackers by your bedside and eat a few before you even lift your head off the pillow. Then lie in bed another 15 or 20 minutes. Allow yourself extra time in the morning. Setting the alarm a little earlier will give you those extra minutes in bed and will keep you from becoming upset and harried. Also try the following:

• Eat lighter meals more often so you're never hungry or overfull.

• Drink liquids after or between meals, not with them.

• Eat and drink slowly.

• Avoid greasy, fried and spicy foods.

• Keep mealtimes calm and peaceful, and rest as often as possible.

• When you feel nauseated, drink club soda, seltzer water, mineral water or some other carbonated beverage.

• Allow plenty of fresh air in the room where you sleep.

• If vomiting is frequent or severe, consult your doctor.

Constipation

A number of factors can contribute to constipation in pregnancy, including hormonal changes, pressure on the lower bowel by the enlarged uterus and iron supplements. Constipation and hard stools may also instigate hemorrhoids or aggravate existing ones. To alleviate the problem, the following suggestions might help:

• Drink plenty of liquids.

• Eat lots of high-fiber foods: whole grains (particularly wheat germ and bran) and raw fruits and vegetables — with skins whenever possible. Dried fruits are also good. Prune juice, prunes, and some other dried fruits are high in iron, too.

• Drink a hot beverage first thing in the morning.

• Get plenty of exercise.

• Do not resort to enemas or laxatives, including mineral oil.

• If the problem continues, talk to your doctor.

Heartburn

During pregnancy, some women are bothered by this form of indigestion, a burning sensation in the lower chest or upper abdomen often accompanied by burping and/or regurgitation of a bit of sour-tasting fluid. An increase or decline in gastric juices, slowed digestion or pressure on the stomach by the growing uterus can be the causes. Avoid antacids, which can cause other problems and may affect some vitamins. Instead, try the following:

- Eat frequent, light meals.
- Limit fatty and spicy foods and rich desserts.
- Eat slowly.
- Drink a bit of cream before meals.
- Get plenty of rest and make meals a peaceful, relaxed time.
- Eat mildly acidic foods like buttermilk and yogurt, which sometimes help.
- Wear clothing that is loose-fitting around the waist.

Cravings

We've all seen the cartoons that picture expectant fathers braving blizzards and storms to fetch ice cream, pickles and anchovy pizzas for their wives. The origins of such cravings are unclear, but they may have to do with hormonal changes playing tricks on your sense of taste. Most cravings can be safely indulged as long as you don't overdo. It's apparently not uncommon for pregnant women to crave non-food items, too (a condition known as pica), including dirt, clay, coal and laundry starch. Don't give in to cravings for such non-foods; doing so can lead to small bowel obstruction, anemia and impaired nutrient utilization. See your doctor if such longings persist.

So much for the problems you *might* experience in pregnancy. Now for the brighter side. Many women report they feel as good or better during pregnancy as they do at any other time. If you're eating correctly, drinking plenty of liquids and getting enough rest and exercise, chances are you'll have no problems. You'll also have the assurance and peace of mind that come from knowing you're giving your baby a solid base for a long, healthy and happy life. And you'll be doing a world of good for yourself at the same time.

Call the Doctor

Any of the following danger signals are reasons to call your physician immediately:

- Vaginal bleeding
- Pain in the abdominal area

- Chills and fever
- Vomiting that will not stop
- Signs of toxemia: blurring of vision, swelling of the face or fingers, bad headaches, sudden weight gain.

Reprinted with permission of the American Medical Association, *Prenatal Care,* copyright 1978, the American Medical Association.

BREAST-FEED YOUR BABY

"No buying, no mixing, no washing, no heating!" Sound like a clever Madison Avenue appeal for yet another high-tech concoction with more substance in the packaging than in the product? Actually, it's a plug for one of the world's oldest and most perfect foods: mother's milk. Unlike many advertising promises, these words from a Center For Science In The Public Interest brochure on breast-feeding understate the advantages of breast-feeding.

A trend away from breast-feeding became popular in the early part of this century, and only in the past decade or so has it begun to reverse. Convenience, snobbery and advertising all combined to make breast-feeding unpopular. Dr. Reba Michels Hill, head of newborn research at St. Luke's Episcopal Hospital and professor of pediatrics at Baylor College of Medicine in Houston, Texas, describes the transition. "When artificial milk became available," she says, "women felt liberated from a duty that encroached on their personal freedom. As recently as 10 years ago, breast-feeding in the United States implied poverty and poor education. Women who breast-fed their infants even in the privacy of their homes or in a ladies' rest room while traveling were stared at and thought to be odd and vulgar. These feelings persisted to some degree through the early 1970s."

Ironically, the better-educated and more financially secure women who first abandoned breast-feeding for commercial formulas have been the first to return. Recent publicity has emphasized its many physiological and psychological benefits. Although only an estimated 18 percent of American women were nursing their babies in 1955, the National Research Council estimates that one-half or more of newborn infants are now being breast-fed.

Even the commercial formula companies have adopted a policy banning advertising that might discourage mothers from breast-feeding. As Ross Laboratories (makers of Similac) literature says, "Breast-feeding is best and is recommended for as long as possible. Breast milk provides the special nutrition babies need."

So, breast-feeding, which has been wholeheartedly endorsed by the World Health Organization, the International Pediatric Association, the American Academy of Pediatrics, the Canadian Pediatric Society and myriad other agencies, is definitely on the rise. Is it just another health and fitness fad or a good idea whose time has come — again? Most important, is it something *you* should do?

MAKING UP YOUR MIND

Whether to nurse your baby is something parents must decide without coercion from well-meaning friends, family, doctors or books. Even though dad has an equal say in how the baby will be nourished, you, the mother will ultimately be doing the feeding. You must be motivated by the prospect of breast-feeding and comfortable with the process. If you're not, it probably won't work out, no matter how badly everyone else may want you to do it.

On the other hand, if the father objects to breast-feeding — whether because of lingering cultural attitudes or subliminal squeamishness, because he feels excluded either from your attention or from the process of nurturing the baby, or for any other reason — chances are you will have a difficult time of it, too. If you are both enthusiastic about it, however, you're almost assured of success.

You should talk over your decision to breast-feed with your husband ahead of time to make sure neither of you has any problems with it that will cause tension or conflict later. You should

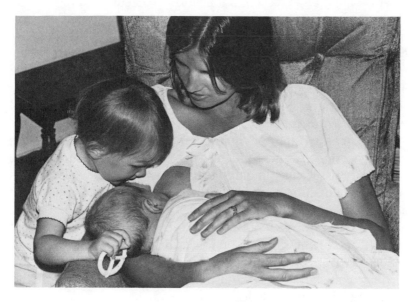

Breast-feeding is a baby's way of gaining essential nutrients and is part of the bonding process between mother and child.

decide as early in your pregnancy as possible, not after the baby is born. An early decision will allow you to become informed about the process and to prepare for it. If your mind is made up and you are prepared, you can begin to feed almost immediately after delivery, which is conducive to plentiful milk production.

Choose an obstetrician/gynecologist and a pediatrician who favor breast-feeding and will support your decision, encouraging you during difficult times and giving you the instruction and information you need. One of the biggest keys to success is a hospital staff that doesn't routinely formula-feed infants or limit the mother's access to her baby. The ideal hospital permits the "on-demand" feeding vital to successful nursing. According to a joint report of the nutrition committees of the American Academy of Pediatrics and the Canadian Pediatric Society, "To enable the new mother to breast-feed, she needs free access to her infant, knowledgeable help, encouragement and instruction. Recent studies have shown a dramatic increase in breast-feeding with in-hospital instruction from staff and mothers. Ninety-six percent of the mothers were able to breast-feed successfully when circumstances were favorable."

There are many excellent publications you can read to learn all you need to know about breast-feeding — from preparing your nipples to holding the baby properly — before the big day comes. Many of them are listed at the back of this book. For more information and support, contact the La Leche League in your area. This organization of nursing mothers and former nursing mothers encourage one another and provide some of the best and most useful information on the subject.

When making up your mind, remember that breast size has nothing to do with successful nursing. Large breasts simply have more fatty tissue surrounding the mammary glands where milk is produced. Small breasts are just as productive. Likewise, nipple shape (particularly inverted nipples) should not hinder you if you are properly informed and prepared. Speak to your doctor and consult one of the suggested publications. No matter what your shape, size or age, if you are relaxed and confident about breast-feeding, you should have no problem producing enough milk to feed your baby in the style nature intended.

BREAST MILK IS BETTER

Although milk from all mammals is composed of the same basic ingredients — water, proteins, fats, sugars and vitamins — every species is unique and so is milk the females produce to feed their offspring. The ideal food for human infants during their first four to six months, when they experience their most rapid growth and their nutritional requirements are very precise, is human milk. And afterward, breast milk is also an excellent supplement to other foods. Our ancestors instinctively knew what to feed a baby, and we are finally coming to the same conclusion.

The nutritional content of human milk varies significantly during the time an infant is being nursed. For example, colostrum, the thick, yellowish fluid produced by women prior to and immediately after delivery, is richer in protein than milk collected after 30 days of lactation.

Likewise, the composition of breast milk changes even during the course of a single feeding. It contains less fat in the initial "fore milk" than in the richer "hind milk" the baby gets near the end of a meal. One study suggests that changes in the taste and texture of human milk as an infant nurses may signal it to stop feeding, enabling the baby to develop a built-in appetite-control mechanism. Infants fed formula would not develop this same mechanism because the composition of the milk remains the same throughout a feeding.

Perhaps that's why breast-fed babies are leaner in infancy and maybe even throughout life. First, while a breast-fed baby determines for itself when it is full and the mother really has little idea how much milk was consumed, the parent with a half-full bottle in his or her hand may worry that the child isn't getting enough and prod it to drink more. Secondly, formula-fed infants are likely to be introduced to solid foods — and potentially more calories — at an earlier age.

One of the most important qualities of mother's milk is the immunity to disease it provides the newborn infant, whose own immune system is immature. Through her milk, the mother passes to her child antibodies to fend off illnesses that can threaten a baby's health in the early months. Substances in the milk may also speed maturation of the infant's own immune system and intestinal tract, where bacterial infections usually take hold. Despite the development of formulas closely matching the composition of breast milk, the antibodies in the real thing have not been duplicated.

Particularly rich in antibodies is the colostrum that precedes milk production by a few days. Babies who are fed it are protected against specific diseases even if they don't nurse after the first few days. According to Karen Pryor in *Nursing Your Baby,* "The first feedings of colostrum may in effect sweep the infant's gastrointestinal tract clean of infectious organisms, giving the baby a real running start."

Continued breast-feeding provides ongoing protection against viral and bacterial infections. The mother's antibodies not only search out and destroy harmful organisms, but help protect against foreign proteins that can trigger allergies. According to an American Academy of Pediatrics report, "Breast milk spares the gastrointestinal tract from exposure to foreign food antigens at a time when macromolecules may be readily absorbed and may cause a local reaction. Evidence suggests that allergic manifestations later in childhood (such as eczema, rhinitis and asthma) are more prevalent in bottle-fed infants than in breast-fed infants, presumably because of the early exposure to cow's milk and other food antigens." Substances in mother's milk also guard against digestive disorders that can be critical in infancy, helping establish a favorable environment for beneficial bacteria in the digestive tract.

Evidence indicates breast-feeding lessens the severity of some serious infantile illnesses and may even prevent them. These diseases include respiratory infections and severe infection-induced vomiting and diarrhea, allergies, infant botulism (linked to crib death or sudden infant death syndrome), and an often fatal intestinal disorder called necrotizing enterocolitis. There is also convincing evidence that throughout childhood breast-fed infants continue to have a much lower incidence of such ailments as ear infections, colds, tonsillitis, diarrheal infections, allergies, and even cavities. Even more amazing, breast-feeding in infancy may confer lifelong health benefits never before suspected.

There is no food better suited to a baby's developing digestive system or more accurately programmed to meet its needs than mother's milk. It provides the correct proportion of necessary nutrients in a form readily digestible. There is no need for baby to overeat to become satisfied and nourished. The makeup of breast milk differs from cow's milk and soy formulas in several ways:

Protein

Whole milk contains about three times the protein of breast milk. Sounds like a plus, but it isn't. Most of that protein is casein, which is poorly digested by the human infant (it forms large, tough curds in the stomach), while breast milk is much richer in easily digestible whey protein. The protein in cow's milk is absorbed only half as efficiently as in human milk. Aside from potential digestive problems, the high protein content of cow's milk may also account for poor absorption of iron and calcium.

The amino acid composition of the protein in human milk differs from formulas and, according to the American Academy of Pediatrics, "is particularly suited to the metabolic peculiarities of the newborn infant." Breast milk has about 30 to 40 times as much of the amino acid taurine as cow's milk. Commercial formulas contain almost no taurine and soy-based formulas contain none. Studies by Dr. Gerald E. Gaull, professor of pediatrics at Mount Sinai Medical Center in New York and a pediatric researcher at the New York State Institute for Basic Research in Mental Retardation, indicate that taurine may play a vital role in brain development. And there is evidence that the taurine supply in breast milk may also affect how a child's body handles cholesterol. There is evidence indicating that babies who are breast-fed for as little as two months may have lower serum cholesterol levels throughout life.

Fat and Cholesterol

Fats are essential to an infant's diet because they contribute the most calories during the baby's period of rapid growth. Breast milk and cow's milk are about equal in total fat content, but cow's milk must be diluted in formulas to make it tolerable for infants, so intake of both calories and fat-soluble vitamins may be reduced. The type of fat differs, too. The fat in human milk is largely unsaturated, while in cow's milk it's mostly saturated. The implications for infant and adult health are currently under investigation.

Fats from breast milk are better absorbed by infants than fats in formulas (probably due to the presence of the enzyme lipase), even when the butterfat in formulas is replaced by vegetable oils. The high polyunsaturated fatty acid content of most infant formulas may also result in a vitamin E deficiency in some infants, although most formulas are adequately fortified. The consequences of feeding infants formulas with fat compositions that differ from mother's milk are not yet known.

Cow's milk has less cholesterol than breast milk and marketed formulas have none. Don't jump to conclusions, though. According to a Canadian Pediatric Society report, "The ingestion of cholesterol during infancy may induce enzymes which may ensure better subsequent cholesterol metabolism and result in lower serum cholesterol later in life." Cholesterol may also play a role in protecting the infant against harmful organisms in the intestinal tract.

Vitamins and Minerals

Cow's milk contains more calcium and phosphorus than breast milk, but much of it is bound to the tough-to-digest protein casein, so those minerals are better absorbed from the latter. Thus, breast-fed babies actually have higher serum calcium levels.

Although all milk is low in iron and may result in anemia if used as the sole source of nutrition for too long, breast milk has slightly more of this mineral than cow's milk. Furthermore, data suggest that more of the iron in human milk — about 50 percent — is absorbed. Thus, breast-fed infants are less likely to develop iron deficiencies than ones who are fed formulas. The difference may be because breast milk contains less protein and phosphorus and more lactose and vitamin C than cow's milk. Infant formulas now have these advantages, too, and the heat treatment used in making them has improved their iron absorption.

It has been suggested that the low iron content of breast milk is intentional, since two iron-binding proteins present — lactoferrin and transferrin — may lose their ability to destroy bacteria when saturated with iron. (This may be an additional drawback of iron-fortified commercial formulas.) Despite the apparent low iron concentration in breast milk, however, infants are born with an adequate store of iron (unless the mother was extremely anemic during pregnancy). Coupled with the iron absorbed from breast milk, the amount is sufficient to meet their needs for four to six months or longer. Formula-fed babies generally need iron supplements by the third or fourth month in the form of liquid, an iron-laced commercial formula or iron-rich solid food.

Mother's milk contains several times the amount of some vitamins and other minerals in cow's milk and less of others. One of the magical properties of breast milk, however, is that although it may not contain as much of a particular vitamin or mineral, it rarely causes vitamin and mineral deficiencies, even when malnutrition of the general population is rife. The implication seems to be that the composition of breast milk is so perfectly suited to the infant's system that absorption and utilization of nutrients easily satisfy a baby's requirements. Often, too, the low levels of particular nutrients are beneficial (as in the case of iron) because a greater concentration would interfere with the absorption and/or work of other vital nutrients.

While the Academy of Pediatrics recommends vitamin C and D (and possibly additional K beyond the single prophylactic dose routinely administered at birth) supplements for breast-fed babies, there is strong evidence that even these vitamins may be present in more than adequate supply in the average mother's milk. Unlike most formulas, breast milk appears to supply enough of the necessary nutrients to be an infant's sole source of nourishment for its first six months.

BREAST-FEEDING BENEFITS MOTHER, TOO

You've just read a few of the ways that breast-feeding benefits your baby. During pregnancy, your body undergoes changes that enable you to nurse your child. You're already prepared for it;

it's the natural next step. If you need further convincing, let's discuss what breast-feeding can do for you.

One common extension of natural or prepared childbirth is the first nursing of the baby right on the delivery table. The baby's sucking stimulates release of the hormone oxytocin, which not only stimulates the release of milk from the mammary glands into the milk ducts that exit through the nipple, but also induces contractions of the uterus. The contractions may serve to expel the placenta, if that hasn't already occurred, as well as control hemorrhaging and promote early healing of the uterine lining. So effective is the process, apparently, that in instances in which the mother is heavily drugged or early nursing is discouraged, a synthetic form of oxytocin, called pitocin, is sometimes administered to do the job. Nursing mothers experience milder contractions at subsequent feedings, which cause the uterus to return to its pre-pregnancy size earlier.

Mother, too, can return to her pre-pregnancy size more quickly and easily with the help of breast-feeding. According to nutrition writer Jane Brody, "Nature provides some 35,000 calories of stored fat — 10 pounds worth — to support milk production, and the mother who doesn't nurse has to lose this fat on her own. At least one study showed that mothers who nursed lost more weight during the first three months after childbirth than those who fed their babies formula."

There are also indications that breasts of mothers who nurse may improve in shape and retain their shape for a longer time. Furthermore, breasts that have been used for their intended purpose — nursing — may be more resistant to cancer. Even a short period of breast-feeding may help, but one study indicates that the one-in-25 breast-cancer rate drops to one in 125 for women who nurse for six months.

Breast-feeding also delays the onset of menstruation, and while it's certainly not a sure-fire method of birth control (you should use something other than the pill), the reduced blood loss relieves the strain on your already overtaxed iron reserves.

Breast milk is also inexpensive (even though you consume more calories and thus buy more food, you spend a fraction of what you do for formulas), safe (always sterile and mixed in the right proportions) and convenient (always available and at the right temperature). Moreover, it makes for a baby who is healthier and happier by cementing the relationship between mother and child. A report of the Canadian Pediatric Society makes this interesting observation:

"Early and prolonged contact between a mother and her newborn baby has been shown to be an important factor in mother-infant bonding and in the development of a mother's subsequent behavior to her infant. Mothers who have had prolonged physical [skin] contact with their newborn infants show, a month later, greater soothing behavior, engage in more eye-to-eye contact and fondling, and are more reluctant to leave their infants with someone else than mothers who had the lesser amount of contact, which is now traditional in maternity hospitals. Breast-feeding tends to promote maternal-infant bonding."

AN EQUAL MIX OF INSTINCT AND INSTRUCTION

If you've made your decision to breast-feed early, and everything goes according to plan, you'll be ready to begin almost as soon as the baby is born. You already know some of the benefits of an early start (controlled bleeding and faster healing of the uterus), but a bigger plus is an invaluable head start in milk production. Breast-feeding is strictly a supply-and-demand business: the more your baby nurses, the more milk you produce. There are many benefits to starting as soon as you and the baby are able.

As already mentioned, it is the baby's sucking that actually stimulates the hormone responsible for the "let-down reflex" that makes milk available at the nipple. Without early and frequent stimulation, milk production will not be as efficient as it should be. Not only will early nursing allow your baby to take advantage of the colostrum that is rich in antibodies, protein and minerals, but it will expedite the production of "real" milk. Frequent nursing will also help prevent such problems as breast engorgement, soreness and infection.

Your doctor may advise you to prepare for breast-feeding sometime during your fifth month by massaging your nipples or rubbing them daily with a washcloth or towel to toughen the skin and prevent soreness later on. You should invest in some well-fitting, supportive bras. Your doctor and his staff should advise you about preparation of your breasts and about their care before delivery and after nursing begins.

Ideally, you should be supervised in your first feeding and coached in such mechanics as proper sitting position and introducing baby to the breast. Some things you will know instinctively; others are better with a little instruction. One thing is certain, though; you will become more proficient at breast-feeding with each passing day. Following are some general guidelines for breast-feeding.

Begin as soon as both you and baby are able — the sooner the better. Relax and try not to be anxious about how you are doing or whether the baby is getting enough. Both of you are new at this, so the first few times may not seem as successful as you hoped. The baby was born with enough body reserves to see it through several days, so don't be alarmed if it doesn't seem to get much at first. Feed the baby as often as it wishes, which will probably be every two or three hours at first, gradually decreasing to perhaps four or five feedings a day by the age of three months or so.

Some doctors suggest limiting initial feedings to between three and five minutes to avoid soreness of inexperienced nipples. Others, contending that a time limit will only delay soreness, suggest letting baby call the shots. Chances are you won't need to go longer than 10 minutes per side. Generally, the let-down reflex takes two or three minutes to come into play, but it may occur more quickly as you become more experienced. You want that to happen so baby can drink both the calorie-rich hind milk (about 35 calories per ounce) and the thinner fore milk (about 35 calories per ounce). Although many babies will want to nurse longer, most of the actual feeding takes places in the first seven to 15 minutes at each breast. Use both breasts at each feeding. To facilitate emptying, begin each feeding with the breast you used last.

At one month or so you may want to introduce the baby to a bottle so you can be away from home for an occasional feeding and so dad can join in the fun by feeding the baby once a day. You can fill the bottle with formula, but it's better for you and baby if you use your own breast milk, which can be expressed by hand or pump and stored in the refrigerator until feeding time. Mothers who return to work while still nursing find that supplying the babysitter with a bottle of breast milk for the missed midday feeding is convenient and keeps milk production up. Breast milk in a sterile container can be stored in the refrigerator for 24 hours, in a refrigerator freezer for two weeks, and longer in the deep freeze (0 degrees).

Follow your doctor's recommendations regarding supplementation for the baby. He will probably prescribe vitamin D and perhaps flouride if the water in your area is not flouridated. Despite any reading you do or advice you receive from health food store clerks or others, don't give your child any vitamins or minerals not prescribed by the doctor.

Your baby may be satisfied more quickly than you think possible, and may indicate so in any number of ways, from unclenching his fists to falling asleep. The baby is the best judge; you may offer the breast once more, but don't insist that he nurse longer.

Breast-fed babies generally gain weight more slowly at first than bottle-fed ones (which is not undesirable), so don't be alarmed if your infant isn't the roly-poly butterball we've come to accept as a "healthy" baby. If a child is overweight in infancy, he may be overweight for the rest of his life. If, however, your baby seems to be losing weight, is irritable, wets only a diaper or two a day or has unusual bowel movements (remember, though, that it's normal for breast-fed babies to have a bowel movement as often as every feeding or as infrequently as every few days), consult the doctor. In any case, you should visit your pediatrician regularly to monitor growth and general health.

RECIPE FOR MILK PRODUCTION

In the midst of all of the attention directed toward baby, remember to look after your own nutrition. If you nurse your baby for six months, you will produce approximately 100 pounds of milk, which is no easy feat and perhaps a bigger drain on your bodily reserves than building a baby. You have to take extra care with your diet during this time, paying special attention to what you eat to produce a nutritious product and maintain your own health. In some ways, your body is designed to take care of the baby's needs at any cost and pulls vital vitamins and minerals into milk production, even if it means leaving you in short supply. The solution is to make sure you get enough of everything for both you and baby.

The board that sets the Recommended Dietary Allowances estimates that the average nursing woman needs to consume somewhere in the neighborhood of 2500 calories a day — 500 more than she needs normally and 200 more than are called for during pregnancy. Actually, the estimated need for extra calories during lactation is 750, but the fat stores you acquired in pregnancy take care of about 250 of those, helping you shed those extra pounds. If you continue to breast-feed for more than three months or so, or gave birth to twins, your energy needs will be greater still, some say as high as an additional 1200 calories per day. Your level of activity will, of course, help determine exactly how much you can and should eat. If you've ever counted calories, you know that 500, while it may sound like a lot, isn't really that much additional food, particularly if it's accounted for by calorically dense sweets, soft drinks and snacks. The trick, as during pregnancy, is to get the most for your calories.

Although breast-feeding doesn't demand as much protein as pregnancy, your needs are still greater than normal — 64 grams a day. Continue eating three or more protein servings a day and remember to emphasize grains, vegetables and legumes rather than high-fat animal sources. Here are some guidelines:

• Increase dairy servings to five per day to provide enough calcium and other micronutrients. Use non-fat and low-fat products. Drink milk fortified with vitamins A and D.

• Eat four or five servings of whole-grain breads, cereals and pastas. These are good sources of many B vitamins, vitamin E and iron.

• Consume plenty of vitamin- and mineral-rich fruits and vegetables. Because of their low calorie content, these can be plentiful in the diet and are your best sources of A, C and folacin. Two servings rich in each of those three (for a total of six), would also cover many of your other needs. A stroll in the sunlight everyday will help both you and baby get enough vitamin D.

• Strict vegetarians (who consume no eggs or dairy products) *must* take B_{12} supplements in order to nurse. A deficiency of it in your milk can cause irreversible harm to your child. Consult your doctor regarding this or any other unusual eating habits.

As in pregnancy, vitamin megadoses during lactation can be toxic to the infant. Your doctor will probably advise you to continue taking your iron supplement (whether or not you nurse) and your vitamin/mineral tablet if you were taking one. He may even suggest more calcium. Do not exceed the doses recommended for you or supplement them with other vitamins.

More liquids are necessary for adequate milk production and to prevent dehydration. You should drink about three quarts a day, which can include your quart of non-fat milk and any soups, juices and water. Make a point of drinking a big glass of water before you sit down to nurse.

Chances are that baby will "eat" anything you eat, but occasionally a mother will notice that certain foods she eats disagree with her child. A particular food may give her milk a flavor the baby doesn't like or cause indigestion or diarrhea. Often, the foods that bother you (perhaps onions, cabbage or hot or spicy foods) will bother the baby. It takes from four to six hours for food you consume to affect your milk. If certain foods you eat seem to upset the baby, eliminate them temporarily. Occasionally, a breast-fed baby develops an allergy to proteins in the milk products his mother consumes. In such cases, the mother must eliminate those foods and take calcium supplements or rely on other sources of calcium. If you suspect such an allergy in your child, consult your doctor.

You should not gain weight during lactation (unless you want to). If you do, you are consuming too many calories (or aren't getting enough exercise) and should cut down sensibly or else increase your activity. Do not cut out wholesome foods, and don't embark on a fad diet or any kind of radical weight-loss program.

Many doctors recommend that the mother drink a small glass of wine or beer before nursing to help relax her and stimulate the let-down reflex, and to assuage any discomfort from sore nipples. Imported beer is richer in B vitamins than domestic brands. Consult your doctor regarding this issue . . . and don't overdo.

As during pregnancy, you shouldn't smoke during lactation. Not only do nicotine and other harmful substances enter your breast milk, but smoking has been shown to hinder milk production. Infants of smokers are also at greater risk of respiratory illness and accidental burns.

Consult your doctor about the ingestion of any drugs while you are nursing — over-the-counter or prescription. Some can accumulate quickly in an infant's system and produce harmful effects, including addiction. Remember, too, that caffeine is a drug, a potentially harmful one that an infant can't get rid itself of easily. In general, it's wise to forego caffeine-rich beverages and foods, but an occasional indulgence is fine a few hours before nursing.

DRUGS IN BREAST MILK

Almost any drug you take will appear in your milk. Following are just a few examples:

Alcohol	Hormones
Amphetamines	Laxatives
Analgesics (pain relievers)	Lead (prevalent in bone meal)
Anesthetics	and other metals
Antibiotics	Methadone
Antihistamines	Minerals
Aspirin	Narcotics
Barbiturates	Nicotene
Caffeine	Tranquilizers
Cortisone	Vitamins

Unbeknownst to you, some potentially harmful chemicals can show themselves in breast milk. Although some dangerous industrial chemicals and pesticides (like PCBs and DDT) have been banned or restricted, they are still present in the environment and can show up in breast milk. Some critics use that as a reason to discourage breast-feeding, but remember that such chemicals also appear in cow's milk, and formulas generally contain some chemical additives. There are ways to reduce your intake of harmful chemicals if you plan to breast-feed. Limit your consumption of animal fats (where chemicals are stored), wash fruits and vegetables carefully, and don't use pesticides (house and garden bug sprays, for example). If you work around chemicals or did at one time — particularly lead, mercury, pesticides and chemicals used in dry cleaning and the manufacture of plastics — consult your doctor about the wisdom of breast-feeding. It is possible to test your breast milk for safety.

Two of the most important ingredients for successful milk production are rest and freedom from stress. Relax, take naps, get plenty of fresh air and exercise; in short, be good to yourself. You'll probably spend three hours or more breast-feeding each day. Sit back and enjoy this quiet and restful time. Anything else can wait, or be done by someone else. This is when a new father comes in real handy. You áre performing a vital task that only you can do, which is much more important than a sinkful of dirty dishes or an unironed shirt. You are not only nourishing the baby, but you are getting the rest you need at a time when your own body is heavily stressed. Make it clear that you can't do anything else while feeding or be bothered with problems. Read or watch television, if that relaxes you, or just spend the time with baby and father. This is an important period when you'll all get to know each other better.

And here's even more incentive to take it easy during lactation: La Leche League estimates that the money you save by not buying formulas can actually pay for household help during the months you are nursing.

ADVANTAGES OF BREAST-FEEDING

For Baby:

- Provides immunity to disease in infancy and perhaps for life.
- May result in lower cholesterol levels throughout life.
- May prevent allergies.
- Easily digestible; less likely to cause constipation or diarrhea.
- Supplies correct balance of nutrients for optimal development.
- Delays need for solid foods.
- Deterrent to obesity in infancy and perhaps for life.
- Provides warmth, security and closeness.

For Mom and Dad:

- Less expensive than bottle-feeding.
- Convenient; no need to sterilize bottles, mix and heat formula.
- No worry about incorrect mixing, spoilage or contamination with infectious organisms.
- Emotionally satisfying for mother; promotes close relationship with infant; can be close, special time for mom and dad.
- Breast-fed babies spit up less and have soft, odorless stools, so they smell better.

• If begun immediately, breast-feeding helps reduce post-delivery bleeding.

• Uterus shrinks to normal size sooner.

• Weight loss and return to pre-pregnancy body shape occur more quickly.

• Menstrual periods resume later.

• May reduce chances of contracting breast cancer.

• Results in a healthier, happier, better-adjusted baby and adult.

BOTTLE-FEED YOUR BABY

If you can't or don't choose to breast-feed, or you quit early, rest assured your baby will grow and develop normally. Witness the several generations of Americans — probably you among them — who were successfully brought up on the bottle. There is widespread agreement that breast-feeding is best, but today's sophisticated formulas, which take the place of plain old cow's milk, provide an adequate substitute.

Most infant formulas are made from cow's milk that is highly modified. They contain less protein and it is broken down somewhat to be more easily absorbed, and baby's exposure to undigested proteins, which can cause allergies or must be flushed away by immature kidneys, is reduced. The milk undergoes other important transformations as well. Butterfat is replaced by polyunsaturated fats to increase the amount the infant absorbs, and lactose is added to approximate the sugar content of breast milk. Sodium, whose overabundance in cow's milk can severely tax a baby's kidneys, is sharply reduced, and there is a better calcium/phosphorus ratio.

Vitamins that are in short supply in breast milk — namely D and K — are added to cow's milk, making bottle-fed infants less susceptible to deficiencies (although breast-fed babies are usually supplemented with these vitamins, too). Some formulas contain additional iron, but it is not as well-absorbed as the iron in

73

Some mothers choose to feed their babies using a bottle.

mother's milk. And formulas are less rich in many other minerals than milk from the breast.

Also common are formulas based on vegetable protein (usually soy), which are often fed to infants whose families have a history of allergy to cow's milk, as well as to those rare infants who manifest an allergy to breast milk. While the fat in these formulas is derived from vegetable oils, the carbohydrates come from sucrose and corn syrup. Some infants who cannot tolerate lactose can be fed formulas that are free of it, and there are also specialized formulas for infants with other disorders.

One thing infant formulas have that breast milk doesn't is food additives to thicken, emulsify and preserve. Many experts, although contending that the additives are probably harmless, view them as an unknown quantity one doesn't have to worry about with breast milk. Two medical researchers from the University of Southern California, Dr. Paul Fleiss and Dr. Jay Gordon, are more adamant. According to them, the two most dangerous additives commonly found in formulas are carrageenan and coconut oil. The doctors believe the former may increase an infant's susceptibility to an often-fatal digestive-tract disorder called necrotizing enterocolitis, while the latter contributes to the formation of lesions associated with arteriosclerosis.

Of the three types of commercial formulas, the powdered varieties are the least expensive. They require only mixing with sterilized water. Higher in cost are the concentrated varieties that are mixed one to one with water. Most expensive are the ready-to-use brands that need no mixing with water. These come either in cans from which the formula can be poured directly into baby's bottle, or, for the ultimate in convenience, particularly when away from home, glass jars that need only have a nipple attached. Needless to say, you pay even more for that kind of convenience.

For less money, and as a way of avoiding additives, you can prepare formulas at home with whole or evaporated milk. According to a Food and Nutrition Board Committee on Nutrition of the Mother and Preschool Child, evaporated-milk formulas made with added sugar and vitamins are less expensive than powdered and concentrated commercial formulas, but home-prepared, whole-milk formulas may or may not be. They beat out ready-to-feed preparations, though. Because of the sometimes marginal cost difference, the fact that prepared formulas are sterilized, provide less opportunity for error in mixing and more closely approximate breast milk, the majority of today's parents prefer to go that route.

If you do choose to prepare your own formula, remember the following:

• Prepare the formula precisely according to doctor's instructions without variations or substitutions. Never fill an infant's bottle with whole cow's milk or undiluted evaporated milk. Even when diluted, these alone are inadequate foods for a baby.

• Do not use skim or non-fat milk in preparing formula; it, too, is inadequate for babies. Non-fat milk doesn't provide enough calories, lacks certain essential fatty acids and contains too much protein, sodium and several other minerals. Likewise, when baby begins drinking from a cup, you should use breast milk or formula until the baby is between nine months and one year old, and then whole milk until about age two. By two years (or when your doctor advises), when baby doesn't require the energy of milk fat, it's time to start thinking about his fat intake and switch to skim.

The Committee on Infectious diseases of the American Academy of Pediatrics strongly advises against using raw (unpasteurized) milk for infants and children. Claims that raw milk is more palatable and nutritionally superior are unproven, and it could cause bacterial intestinal disease. The Committee urges parents to be aware "of the dubious benefits and important risks inherent in the consumption of raw milk, and endorses pasteurized milk whenever whole milk is prescribed for infants and children."

Infant formulas are now packed in lead-free cans, but evaporated-milk cans are sealed with a lead solder plug, which makes evaporated milk higher in lead than either infant formula or cow's milk. Because of their size, infants are particularly susceptible to a build-up of toxic levels of lead. Convincing evidence has linked lead with childhood learning and behavioral problems. The amount of ingested lead in any diet should be minimal, but especially in those of infants and pregnant and nursing women.

Before the baby is one year old: never add honey to infant formula; never feed a baby a mixture of honey and water; never spread honey on your nipple to induce a child to take a bottle. Some honey contains botulism spores that can colonize in the intestines and produce botulinal toxin, the most deadly poison known. Honey has been shown to be one cause of infant botulism, which in turn has been linked to sudden infant death syndrome (SIDS), commonly known as crib death.

One of the biggest problems with formulas of any kind — store-bought or homemade — is the possibility of overfeeding. Although breast-fed babies generally decide for themselves when they have had enough (the composition of the milk itself may cue them when to stop), bottle-fed babies often don't have that option and are prodded by well-meaning parents into finishing each and every bottle. Perhaps it's our Puritan ethic that makes us hesitate to waste food, or a fear that the baby will starve; whatever, the result could be obesity, both immediately and in the future. Like the breast-fed infant, the one who takes a bottle should have the option of eating whenever he's hungry and stopping whenever he's full. If a baby prefers to sleep occasionally instead of eat or just doesn't want to eat at a scheduled feeding, that's okay.

Generally, bottle-fed babies eat less often than breast-fed ones. Feedings may be spaced every three or four hours rather than every two or three, for a total of six to eight meals a day. As the baby's stomach capacity increases (it can hold just two tablespoons at birth), feedings should be spaced even further apart.

Nutrition writer Jane Brody also offers this sage advice: "Don't shove a bottle in the baby's mouth at every cry. Babies cry for a lot of reasons — soiled diaper, need for suckling or cuddling, gas, thirst — not just for hunger. *Try other pacifiers first, including a bottle of water, before offering food if it's not a regular feeding time.*"

Following are some more guidelines for preparing and feeding formulas:

• Follow the doctor's advice regarding the type of formula, how much to feed and so on. If you aren't using a ready-to-feed formula, follow package instructions precisely. Often, more water is added to formula for newborns than for older infants, so mix according to the doctor's specifications. Never attempt to "stretch" formula with extra water, which can rob baby of essential nutrition, and do not add any supplements that have not been specifically prescribed.

• Bottle-fed babies may need more water to rid their bodies of the greater solute load of artificial formulas. Keep bottles of sterilized water on hand, especially in hot weather when babies lose a lot through evaporation.

• Do not buy or use infant formula after the date that appears on the top of the can.

• Before opening a can of liquid formula, wash the top of the can with soap and hot water, rinse and dry. Use a clean, punch-type (sometimes called "church key") opener to make two small, uniform holes. Open a can of powdered formula with an electric or hand opener that is clean, sharp and free from rust.

• An opened can of powdered formula can be stored in a cool, dry place up to four weeks.

• Opened liquid can be stored, covered, up to 48 hours in the refrigerator.

• A bottle of formula may remain safely at room temperature up to three hours before it is fed to the baby.

• Because some formula that touches the baby's mouth returns to the bottle, and because bacteria grow rapidly, any formula left in the bottle after a feeding should be discarded. Dr. Spock says, however, that if the baby habitually falls asleep halfway through a bottle and wakes in an hour or two to finish it, place the unfinished portion in the refrigerator promptly and it will be safe to reuse for the second half of the meal. Do not reuse it after that, however.

• When you open a can of ready-to-feed formula that has been stored at room temperature, you don't need to heat it.

• Bottles of refrigerated formula should be heated on the stove in a pan of water until just warm, not hot. Test the temperature by shaking a few drops onto the inside of your wrist. Ross Laboratories (makers of Similac) caution that microwave ovens should never be used for heating infant formula because even though the bottle may remain cool, the formula can become extremely hot.

Today, thanks to pre-sterilized formulas (which often come in single-serving cans), relatively clean tap water, generally high standards of hygiene, and the prevalence of electric dishwashers that use very hot water, the big job of sterilizing bottles is considered by many to be obsolete. Bottles are now commonly filled one at a time as they are used, following the rationale that bacteria left in the bottle from the last feeding won't have time to multiply before baby drinks the formula. Bottles used this way should be either carefully scrubbed with a brush, soap and hot water or washed in a dishwasher. Nipples should be cleaned out carefully with a nipple brush and boiled in a pan on the stove. They may be stored in a clean jar until used.

If you do wish to prepare a day's worth of bottles ahead of time or if your doctor advises sterilization, the best methods are outlined step-by-step in a number of publications, including the old standby, Dr. Spock's *Baby And Child Care, The Better Homes And Gardens New Baby Book,* and a Ross Laboratories publication called *How To Formula-Feed Your Baby.* Whichever method of bottle preparation you choose, baby's formula and its containers should be prepared with the utmost care and cleanliness to avoid the possibility of contamination that makes bottle-feeding somewhat riskier than breast-feeding.

As a final note, remember that bottle-feeding has one clear advantage over breast-feeding: It allows dad to get in early on the

Comparison of Milk Sources

Type	Calories* per fluid ounce	Grams protein per quart	Grams fat per quart
Breast milk	20	10	43
Commercial formula	20	14	34
Whole cow's milk	20	32	36
2% Low-fat cow's milk	15	32	19
Non-fat (skim cow's) milk	11	33	2

*Babies need to consume approximately 50 calories per day for each pound of weight. Figures are approximate.
Source: *Nutrition, Growth and Development During Your Baby's First Year,* Ross Laboratories, Columbus, Ohio. December 1983.

Nutritional Content of Selected Milk Products

	Calories	Protein (grams)	Fat (grams)	Carbo-hydrates (grams)	Calcium (grams)	Iron (mg)	Sodium (mg)	Vitamin A (IU)	Thiamine (mg)	Riboflavin (mg)	Niacin (mg)	Vitamin C (mg)
Mother's milk, 1 cup	192	2.4	9.6	23.2	80	trace	40	560	trace	.08	.8	16
Whole milk, (raw or pasteurized), 1 cup	159	8.5	8.5	12.0	288	.1	122	350	.07	.41	.2	2
Low-fat milk, 1 cup	145	10.3	4.9	14.8	352	.1	150	200	.1	.52	.2	2
Non-fat milk, 1 cup	88	8.8	.2	12.5	296	.1	127	10	.09	.44	.2	2
Canned, evaporated milk, 1 cup	345	17.6	19.9	24.4	635	.3	297	810	.10	.86	.5	3
Instant dry milk (whole), 1 cup	132	6.9	7.2	10.0	239	.1	106	298	.08	.38	.2	1.5
Goat's milk, 1 cup	163	7.8	9.8	11.2	315	.2	83	390	.10	.27	.7	2

Infant Heights and Weights*

Age	Sex	Usual Length Range	Usual Weight Range
Birth	Girl	17¾ in. to 20¾ in.	5 lb. 4 oz. to 8 lb. 8 oz.
Birth	Boy	18¼ in. to 21½ in.	5 lb. 8 oz. to 9 lb. 4 oz.
1 Month	Girl	19¼ in. to 22½ in.	6 lb. 8 oz. to 10 lb. 12 oz.
1 Month	Boy	19¾ in. to 23 in.	7 lb. to 11 lb. 12 oz.
3 Months	Girl	21¾ in. to 25 in.	9 lb. 4 oz. to 14 lb. 12 oz.
3 Months	Boy	22¼ in. to 25¾ in.	9 lb. 12 oz. to 16 lb. 4 oz.

Source: National Center for Health Statistics

*Approximately 90 percent of babies fall into these ranges. Greater or lesser length or weight may be normal or may indicate a nutritional or health problem. These figures should be viewed as guidelines only, not as requirements your baby should fulfill. Your doctor is the best judge of your baby's state of health and nutrition.

act of feeding baby and the cuddling and close contact that go with it. He should take this excellent opportunity and share equally in the feedings. And remember never to leave an infant alone with a propped bottle. Unless the bottle is tilted properly, the baby will consume too much air, and there is also the danger of spitting up or choking. Allowing a baby to go to sleep with a bottle coats the teeth with sugar, which can lead to decay.

FROM BREAST TO SPOON

Telephone lines are buzzing. Mom and dad have called both sets of grandparents and now they are busy phoning their friends and relatives. This is a monumental day marked by an unforgettable occasion: Your baby has just taken his first spoonful of solid food. What may sound like a silly scenario is really closer to the truth than many of us would like to believe. That first bite of cereal, the initial unsteady step, the first garbled word — all are important stages in baby's development and status symbols to new parents. Sometimes mom and dad may even prod the little one to accomplish these feats before he is ready to beat the deadlines on the developmental charts and show what a genius baby is, or to get a jump on the baby down the block.

There are other reasons besides status why solids are introduced to infants too early. Some parents and doctors may feel that the baby isn't receiving enough of certain nutrients — iron, for example — from milk alone or that solid foods will induce him to sleep through the night. Neither is the case, however, nor is it necessary or advisable to introduce solids before the baby has reached 13 to 15 pounds and is *at least* three months old.

The American Academy of Pediatrics says that "There is no known nutritional basis for starting solid foods before three months of age." The Canadian Pediatric Society says that

"There are no absolute guidelines for timing the introduction of solids. In most infants there is no nutritional reason to add solids to feedings before six months of age. Some infants do appear unsatisfied with milk alone by the age of three or four months and then the gradual introduction of solids is not unreasonable." It is generally agreed that solids may be introduced sometime between the fourth and sixth months — the later the better. The date your baby eats solid food depends on whether he is breast-or bottle-fed, on your own observations and your doctor's advice.

There are a number of good reasons to wait until this time to introduce solid foods. First, younger babies are not sufficiently developed. It is not until about the fourth month or so that the baby's "extrusion reflex" begins to disappear. This thrusting movement of the tongue, designed to extract milk from the nipple, can make attempted feedings of solid foods pretty unproductive. As mom or dad spoons in the food, the baby's tongue pushes it right back out again. Until the baby's oral and neuro-muscular development progresses beyond this stage, feeding solids is frustrating for both child and parent. By the age of four months, an infant has usually developed the capacity to move food from the front of the mouth to the throat and then swallow.

Similarly, University of Iowa researchers have observed that it is not until five or six months of age that a baby is "able to indicate desire for food by opening its mouth and leaning forward, and to indicate disinterest or satiety by leaning back and turning away. Until the infant can express these feelings," they say, "feeding solid foods will probably represent a type of forced feeding."

If your baby is being fed breast milk or the recommended formula and is receiving any supplements your doctor has deemed necessary, you accomplish nothing by forcing solid foods before six months, and you may even cause some problems. The baby's digestive system is still immature and premature introduction of solids can lead to gastrointestinal upset or open the door to allergies as substances like proteins pass through the intestinal wall undigested. The kidneys, too, can become overtaxed in trying to rid the body of excess wastes.

Adding solids too soon may lead to obesity, which can become a lifetime pattern and a serious threat to health. Solid foods are much higher in calories than breast milk or formula (not to mention nutritionally inferior), so feeling satisfied (and getting the necessary nutrients) requires the infant to consume more calories and perhaps put on weight. The American Academy of Pediatrics theorizes that besides providing excess calories, feeding solids for other than nutritional reasons "may contribute to the difficulty some older children, adolescents or adults may have in restricting their diet when indicated."

By the age of four or five months, your baby may seem dissatisfied with milk alone or finish a breast or bottle feeding with an "Is that all there is?" look on his face. Once the baby's doctor decides he is ready, the key is to start slowly with no more than an experimental spoonful the first day. Experts concur that the point of these first meals is not significant nutrition from solid foods, but a positive introduction to them and the gradual mastery of a new skill.

What you feed your baby first will depend largely on your pediatrician's preference. The Canadian Pediatric Society contends that "the order of introduction of solid foods is probably of little nutritional consequence," but concedes that grain products, such as pre-cooked, iron-fortified infant cereals are baby's usual entree into the world of adult foods. Rice cereal, mixed with breast milk or formula to the consistency of creamed soup, is preferred because it is the least allergenic.

Parents magazine associate editor Julie Cooper suggests giving the baby about half the breast milk or formula he would normally drink. "Since the first foods must be pureed," she says, "take a small bit of cereal and thin it out with familiar-tasting breast milk or formula. Using a baby spoon, a demitasse spoon, or a small plastic spoon, give the baby a tiny taste, placing the spoon a little bit back on his tongue. For this first meal, feed the baby only one to two teaspoons. You can then offer him more milk if he is still hungry." At first, one or two of these mini-feedings a day is enough. Meanwhile, the bulk of baby's diet should continue to come from that best of all baby foods: breast milk or formula. To give a youngster time to adjust, some experts suggest using a single food — like the rice cereal — for an entire month before adding another; others say one week. Your baby's doctor will have his own opinion.

At any rate, mixed foods (multi-grain cereals, fruit mixed with cereal and the like) should not be offered at first, and new foods should be added one at a time at intervals of several days to a week. That way, allergic reaction or intolerance to foods, characterized by rashes, runny nose, vomiting, diarrhea or cramps, can be noted easily and offensive foods omitted. Try the foods again when your child is a little older. Although fruits are commonly added to baby's diet after cereals (try oats and barley after rice), many experts now agree that vegetables may be a better bet. There is some evidence that vegetables will be better accepted if introduced before fruits, and besides, they are also a better source of protein. You may also begin offering water, which baby needs more of now, breast milk, or formula or fruit juice (either baby juices or diluted adult juices) from a cup. Don't put juices or liquified fruit or cereal in a bottle; doing so can lead to choking, overfeeding or tooth decay and deny baby the learning experience of seeing and feeling the textures of new foods and becoming comfortable with eating from a spoon.

The Canadian Pediatric Society advises adding meats to baby's diet last, "as their higher solute load and protein content is neither needed nor well-tolerated before the age of six months." Most physicians suggest delaying the introduction of highly allergenic foods — including orange juice, wheat, eggs and cow's milk — until at least the seventh month, longer if there is a family history of allergies.

Between six and nine months of age, the baby will progress from pureed to lumpy foods. By then, says the Canadian Pediatric Society, "the infant will be starting to acquire teeth and make meaningful chewing movements, and 'chewable' foods can be started. This is also referred to as the 'sensitive learning period' for chewing and feeding, and delay in the introduction of lumpy foods beyond this age may result in later feeding difficulties."

As baby's skill with and interest in solid food increases, he will increase his intake from a few tablespoons each of cereal, vegetables, fruits and meats in the beginning, to 20 to 30 tablespoons spread over three or four feedings by the end of the first year. With the introduction of solids and liquids from a cup, the gradual process of weaning your baby away from the breast will begin.

As with breast- and bottle-feeding, the baby is the best judge of when he has had enough at a solid-food feeding. When it comes

Children love to play with their food. A piece of carrot will make this doll healthy and strong.

to eating, your goal is to nourish your child adequately, not create a human being who will go through life not knowing when enough is enough.

WHAT TO CONSIDER WHEN INTRODUCING SOLID FOODS

• The extrusion reflex does not disappear until three or four months of age.

• The neuromuscular coordination necessary for swallowing solid foods is not fully developed until four to four and a half months of age.

• For an infant's needs, the nutritional values of solids are inferior to milk.

• Certain solids impose too great a load on a baby's immature kidneys.

• The addition of solids alters the intestinal flora in a breast-fed infant and may diminish the immune protection provided by breast milk.

• By the age of six months, breast milk may not satisfy the infant's protein or caloric needs.

• Six to nine months of age appears to be a critical period for the development of taste and texture preferences.

• Solids can provide supplemental iron and vitamin C after the age of six months.

Source: Canadian Pediatric Society Nutrition Committee, September, 1979.

A WORD ABOUT WATER

• For the most part, infants get enough water from breast milk or formula, but, during hot weather or when fluid losses are high, they may need more of it.

• Infants less than two months of age are especially susceptible to bacterial and viral infections and should receive sterilized (boiled, not distilled) water. Use sterilized water in formulas, too.

• Well water may contain high levels of nitrates and should not be given to infants younger than four months of age. Because there is less acidity in the stomachs of infants, nitrates are easily converted to nitrites in the gastrointestinal tract, and the result can be methemoglobinemia. As Kenda and Williams describe it, methemoglobinemia is a condition in which nitrites "are absorbed into the blood where they combine with hemoglobin, the oxygen-carrying compound within the red blood cells, to form methemoglobin. Methemoglobin interferes with the ability of the red blood cells to carry oxygen and in high amounts would be capable of causing suffocation."

• Infants should not be given softened water, which contains high levels of sodium that can harm an infant's immature kidneys.

• Do not sweeten an infant's drinking water with sugar, syrup or honey. The latter can cause infant botulism and all can predispose an infant to sweets and possibly contribute to the development of "nursing mouth caries," which promotes decay of the early front teeth.

Source: *Feeding Recommendations For Healthy Infants,* Missouri Division of Health.

BABY'S FIRST FOODS

Until now, feeding your baby was straightforward; you either breast- or bottle-fed. But when your baby is old enough to eat solid food, the choices and concerns multiply. Which foods are safe and appropriate? How much should you feed your baby? Is it better to buy commercial baby foods or make your own? What is necessary to provide a balanced diet and meet the baby's nutritional needs? And, perhaps most importantly, how do you establish, at an early age, a lifetime pattern of good eating habits? In some ways, the introduction of solid foods is an orientation period for new parents, preparing them for the tough decisions that lie ahead.

COMMERCIAL BABY FOODS

The baby food industry is one of the most profitable food businesses in the United States. During baby booms, business is even better. The ease of using baby-sized portions already pureed to the correct consistency is largely responsible for the popularity of commercial infant foods.

But there seems to be more to their appeal than convenience. Perhaps it is their "official" look. Or is it our belief that everything given to babies must be specifically manufactured for babies? Whatever their appeal is, most Americans think those

*What mother isn't familiar with baby food
in tiny jars? The small serving portions are
convenient.*

little glass jars on supermarket shelves are the only safe and effective way to feed a baby. That is precisely what the baby food
manufacturers want you to think. But commercial baby foods
have experienced a past as questionable as the convenience food
industry, and they are still aren't perfect.

According to Margaret Elizabeth Kenda and Phyllis S. Williams, authors of *The Natural Baby Food Cookbook,* inflated
food prices after World War II first induced baby food companies "to stretch their meats, vegetables and fruits with sugar
and starch. Then to bring back some of the thinned-out taste,
which must not have smacked enough of the original foods, they
added salt and monosodium glutamate (MSG)." The key ingredients in baby foods came to be water, starch (later it was modified
starch that is indigestible by babies but keeps the product fresh-
looking longer), sugar, salt (five times as much in baby foods
containing meat as in fresh meat; sometimes 60 times as much in

strained vegetables as in their fresh counterparts), and flavor enhancers.

Many of these ingredients were added to stretch the real ingredients in baby food . . . and the profit on it. And some of them were added to improve the taste of overrefined pap to please not babies — because it's been proven they could care less, but parents who taste the food. The principle is the same as for pet foods prepared in cunning shapes and colors to appeal not to dogs and cats, but to their eager-to-please owners.

In 1969, public outcry over tests showing monosodium glutamate (MSG) caused brain damage in infant mice forced the baby food companies to reluctantly but voluntarily stop adding MSG. Interestingly, however, the industry did not pull the MSG-laced infant foods already in stores and warehouses. Thanks to baby food's three-year shelf life, some infants not yet conceived when MSG use was discontinued were still consuming it a few years later.

Putting salt and sugar in infant foods may help babies acquire a taste for those additives. Salt in infant food can not only put an excessive load on young kidneys, but may predispose infants and children to hypertension in later life. This so-called "silent killer" afflicts an estimated 10 to 20 percent of all Americans and can lead to stroke, heart disease and kidney failure. Similarly, sugar adds nothing healthy to infant food but leads to lifelong overconsumption of sweets, unnecessary, empty calories, and contributes to tooth decay, heart disease and diabetes. Neither ingredient should be in baby food, to say nothing of food for older children and adults.

Today, salt is no longer added to strained infant meats and vegetables, though it is still in some junior foods, meat sticks, biscuits and cookies aimed at older infants. Sugar appears in these foods also, as well as in some strained fruits. Often it masquerades as corn syrup, a cheaper form of sugar. Modified starches are prominent ingredients in baby dinners and desserts. Water is still a major ingredient in all commercial baby food. Although water certainly isn't harmful and is necessary in home-prepared foods, you are, so say the authors of *The Natural Baby Food Cookbook,* "paying meat prices for water."

There can be psychological drawbacks to the frequent and/or prolonged use of commercial baby foods. Kenda and Williams contend that once the baby becomes accustomed to these bland, sweet, milky, smoothly textured foods, he may lose the natural curiosity to explore new foods. By the age of two, say the authors, he may want "nothing at all but the long-familiar milk and the cereal and the purees of his junior food jars. He hasn't learned how to chew. He doesn't like strong tastes. He doesn't like spice or variety or strength in his food.

"As he gets even bigger, then, he is liable to like only foods that are bad, bad, bad for him. He will want only the bland flavors created by overrefining, oversweetening, and over-processing.

"What happened to the curiosity, the adventure, the food-exploring of the baby? He forgot them for the tasteless purees, the sugar and the cereal of the commercial jars he emptied too long."

Despite their drawbacks, commercial baby foods are consummately convenient and adequately nutritious. Even if you choose to prepare your own baby food at home, there will be times when you will make use of commercial baby foods. They're ideal for after-work feeding when you have nothing prepared, they're handy to leave with the baby-sitter, and have no peer in safety and convenience when you've got to feed the baby away from home or while traveling. Whether you choose commercial foods on a full-time or, preferably, an occasional basis, here are some guidelines to their selection and use:

Commercial infant cereals are precooked, ready to eat and easy to digest. Although you may want to begin with your own home-cooked cereal, strained and thinned to appropriate consistency, these cereals are suitable substitutes and are fortified with iron, thiamine, riboflavin and niacin. Processing, which causes vitamin loss, is reportedly kept to a minimum.

You should purchase iron-fortified baby cereals in the box rather than premixed in jars. You save a lot of money initially and eliminate waste by mixing only the amount you need — especially important in the beginning, when your baby may eat only a teaspoon or two a day. Buying the boxed variety also gives you the opportunity to mix the cereal with nutritious, familiar-tasting breast milk or formula. At first the cereal should have the thin, watery consistency of creamed soup. As your baby matures, cereal should be made thicker; it should hold its shape on the spoon.

Buy single-ingredient cereals at first (starting with rice, then moving on to barley and oats). Add highly allergenic wheat cereal, or combinations containing wheat, after seven months to one year or as directed by your pediatrician. But check the package label before buying boxed, single-ingredient cereals. One leading brand of rice cereal contains just rice flour, plus assorted vitamins and minerals (including iron), but another contains rice flour, soy oil-lecithin, barley malt flour, and vitamins and minerals.

Premixed cereals contain water, and usually other ingredients (such as fruit and non-fat dry milk), making them unsuitable fare when you want to introduce your baby to only one new food at a time. For example, the contents list on a leading brand of rice cereal with applesauce reads: Water (the main ingredient), apples, non-fat milk, rice flour, sugar, modified corn starch, fully ripened bananas, plus vitamins and minerals.

If you must use commercial baby foods, the strained vegetables and meats are your best bet. They generally contain only the main ingredient (i.e., peas, carrots, pork, veal, etc.) on the label and water. Vegetables can be introduced right after cereals, and you should start with the milder-tasting ones such as carrots, squash and peas. About one month later, you can start your child on infant meats. They're in a form readily accepted by babies, and are a good source of protein, iron and many of the B vitamins. These are a healthier and more economical buy than baby dinners and soups, which are low in protein and diluted with modified starches and more water. Don't buy combinations of any type, because they make it more difficult to single out foods that cause reactions, and generally have more of the inferior, less expensive ingredients. Consider these examples:

• One commercial meat dinner contains: water, beef, rice flour, tomato puree, carrots, wheat flour, potato solids, torula yeast and onion powder.

• Meat sticks designed as finger food for older infants contain: pork and beef, water, turkey meat, calcium-reduced dried skim milk, salt, sugar, garlic powder, extractives of black pepper, thyme, basil and bay.

• The number one ingredient in such baby combinations as vegetables and bacon, mixed vegetables, turkey and rice, and vegetables and beef is water. Despite the names on the label, the second most abundant ingredient is carrots, which cost much less than chicken, turkey, beef, bacon and many vegetables. Carrots are a wholesome food, but babies who consume a regular diet of commercial infant foods get far too many of them. A single jar of strained carrots, for example, contains enough carotene to provide 1000 to 1500 percent of the RDA of vitamin A for infants. Indeed, it is not uncommon for infants regularly consuming commercial carrots and dinners to develop carotene-mia, a high level of carotene in the blood that gives the skin a yellowish cast. The same reaction is possible, of course, if an infant is fed the same amounts in home-prepared food.

Although large doses of preformed vitamin A can be toxic, the Center For Science In The Public Interest reports that "carotene-mia has no known adverse effects, other than turning the skin yellow — and that's reversible. Though the body ordinarily converts carotene to vitamin A, it seems to slow or shut down this conversion mechanism when large amounts of carotene are eaten. Some researchers believe carotene builds up in the skin precisely because it is no longer being converted to vitamin A. In effect, the body refuses to poison itself by converting too much carotene to vitamin A." Thus, according to the center, "While excess carotene is not harmful, it can discolor an infant's skin and frighten parents." To make matters worse, some products have been labeled to show much lower levels of carotene than are present.

If you buy commercial fruits, buy single-fruit varieties with only water and perhaps vitamin C and citric acid added. Citric acid is a natural preservative derived from citrus fruits. Forget about the atrocities known as baby desserts; you don't want your baby to develop a taste for these sweet, starchy non-foods. They come under a variety of guises, including puddings, peach cobbler and various fruits with tapioca to sweeten and extend them. The label on a jar of apricots with tapioca reads: water, apricots from concentrate, corn syrup, modified tapioca starch, vitamin C.

If you buy baby juices — unquestionably convenient but costly — buy the single-fruit variety first and read the label to be sure sugar or corn syrup isn't added. Baby juice is sold in ready-to-use nursing bottles that need only a nipple attached, but also promote tooth decay. Because vitamin C is retained in breast milk and added to commercial formulas, juice is no longer considered necessary in the early months of baby's diet.

Juice should be introduced when your baby is ready to begin drinking from a cup. The American Academy of Pediatrics advises: "The marketing of juices in ready-to-use nursing bottles may tend to prolong bottle feeding and to encourage the use of the bottle as a pacifier, both of which promote dental caries. The use of juices from a bottle should be discouraged; infants should be offered juice from a cup as soon as possible." Water from a cup after a meal — particularly one containing fruit or juice — can help rinse the teeth of these sweet substances.

Some supermarket shoppers have the rude and potentially dangerous habit of opening jars, tasting or smelling their contents, and putting them back on the shelf. It's done with everything from mayonnaise and pickles to jars of baby food.

Baby food jars have a safety feature that indicates whether they have been opened. If the small tab is raised, the airtight seal has been broken and the product should not be purchased.

Once the vacuum seal is broken, bacteria — in particular the sometimes lethal salmonella — begin to multiply rapidly. Fortunately, baby food jars have a built-in warning to indicate when they have been opened. Their lids have a small, circular indent that pops up when the jar is opened. Do not buy or serve a jar of baby food if this safety button is raised.

Unless you plan to use an entire container of baby food or dispose of the remainder, do not heat it in the jar or feed the baby from it. Bacteria introduced from the baby's mouth can multiply rapidly. Remove the portion you plan to feed the baby to another dish; you can then refrigerate the unused portion in the jar for two to three days.

After much public pressure, baby food manufacturers removed the salt and sugar from most of their products. It doesn't matter to the babies for whom the food is intended, but well-meaning parents who taste the food may be alarmed at its blandness and attempt to doctor it to their own tastes by adding these potentially harmful substances. Remember: Saltiness and sweetness are tastes you aren't anxious for your baby to acquire. Do not add salt, sugar, honey (implicated in infant botulism), or other flavorings to commercial baby foods.

Even if you do use strained infant foods, don't graduate your child to "junior" and "toddler" foods. It's time he was eating modified "real" foods consumed by the rest of your family. If you've gone to the trouble of adopting a healthy diet, there's

---

ESTIMATED SAFE AND ADEQUATE DAILY DIETARY INTAKE OF SODIUM*

Age	Sodium (mg)
0 — 6 months	115 — 350
6 months — 1 year	250 — 750
1 — 3 years	325 — 975

*Levels that should not be exceeded.

(Source: Recommended Dietary Allowances, Food and Nutrition Board, National Research Council, 1980).

---

every reason to introduce your little one to it. It's a good idea to get the newest member of your family used to your usual fare early in life. Junior foods have a somewhat chewier texture, but are not a significant step up from the blandness of strained foods except that they are adulterated by sugar and salt. Although your child won't experience any significant chewing or variety of taste and texture, he will get a headstart on unhealthy additives.

But there is no reason to wait until your baby is ready for junior foods to begin weaning him from jars to the fresh, whole foods you consume. You can make your own safe, wholesome infant foods at home right now.

MAKING YOUR OWN BABY FOOD

Making baby food? Isn't that something people did in the 1960s when everybody lived in communes? Today many parents are making baby food at home because it tastes better than commercial baby food, and its broad range of colors and textures gives your baby a healthy interest in good food without additives,

Ice cube trays are ideal for storing small food portions for the baby. Use a blender to puree the food, pour into the ice tray and freeze.

sugar and salt. Homemade baby food is also inexpensive (costing half or less than commercial varieties), perfectly safe, easier to make and less time-consuming than you might imagine. It makes use of the wholesome foods you are already buying for the rest of the family.

Prior to the 1920s, solid foods were seldom given to infants younger than one year of age. That same decade, however, saw the birth of the first, and still largest, commercial baby food concern. Although solid food should be introduced between three and six months, the availability of convenient infant foods and other factors began the trend to stuffing babies with solid food much earlier. If making one's own baby food were a difficult or inconvenient task, parents might hold off feeding solids as long as possible. But home preparation of infant foods — particularly given today's modern gadgetry — couldn't be easier. Here are some general tips to get you started:

Because babies are susceptible to bacteria, work with scrupulously clean hands and cooking utensils.

Home-prepared baby foods made from fresh or frozen fruits, vegetables and meats will taste better than their commercial counterparts. You have no reason to douse them with salt, sugar, fat and other seasonings harmful to the infant.

Immediately refrigerate or freeze any prepared infant foods you won't be serving right away. Homemade baby food can be safely stored covered (baby food jars or small plastic containers are ideal) in the refrigerator for two days. To make life easier — and to ensure that you always have fresh, nourishing food on hand — you can prepare foods in large quantities and freeze them. If you freeze food in small, glass jars, don't fill them to the top. A more popular method is to fill plastic, pop-out ice cube trays with the pureed food and then freeze. The frozen cubes should then be transferred to a covered container or sealed plastic bag labeled with the contents and date. Baby foods can be safely stored one to two months this way.

At mealtime, remove the cubes you need and return the rest to storage. Food to be served can be easily thawed in a double-boiler, small egg poacher, microwave, or heated saucepan with a bit of water in it. Test the food temperature to be sure it is only tepid before serving. Unlike adults, babies will eat cool food;

keep in mind they can be burned by food that may seem warm to us.

As an alternative to freezing food in ice cube trays, you can use the "plop method" outlined by Vicki Lansky in her excellent guide to infant food preparation, *Feed Me! I'm Yours.* She drops spoonfuls of pureed food onto a cookie sheet for freezing. "Plops" are then stored in the same manner as cubes. Both are ideal for short excursions away from home or for taking to the baby-sitter's. Put them in a small jar or container, and by the time your baby's hungry, they should be thawed and ready to eat.

Making food for infants will be much easier with a blender, food processor or baby food grinder, but if you don't mind a little more work you can push soft foods such as liver, egg yolk, fruits and vegetables through a strainer. And consider using a vegetable steamer, the most nutritious way to prepare vegetables for the entire family. Although you can puree virtually any of your regular fare for your baby's consumption, using a pressure cooker or crock pot is a good way to produce tender meats and vegetables.

You'll probably puree small dabs from your regular meals, and you should come up with many interesting and nutritious concoctions of your own. You'll find many tips and recipe ideas for your baby in one of the publications devoted to the home preparation of infant foods. A number of them are listed in the back of this book. One caution, however: Ignore any suggestion to add salt, sugar and especially honey to food given to infants less than a year old.

Cereals

Commercial infant cereals are simple to prepare, finely textured, fortified with iron, and easy to digest. You may find these cereals the best foods to begin feeding your baby. But your little one can also eat the nutritious hot cereals that make an excellent adult breakfast. Most are rich in the iron your baby will begin to need from sources other than breast milk by the age of six months. You may use processed adult cereals such as Cream of Rice, and Farina, Cream of Wheat or Wheatena (when the doctor says it's okay to introduce wheat).

For younger babies, Kenda and Williams suggest cooking

according to package directions and then removing the baby's portion and cooking an additional 15 minutes over boiling water (in a double-boiler or egg poacher). Oatmeal can be made suitable for infants by straining the cooked cereal or by grinding the raw oats in a blender and then cooking as you would normally.

Both Lansky and Kenda and Williams offer suggestions for turning whole grains such as barley and millet into delicious, nutritious baby cereal. *The Deaf Smith Country Cookbook* suggests feeding your baby the "milk" that forms on rice when cooked, or mixing that "milk" with the rice and blending or grinding. The authors also offer easy recipes for baby cereal from whole grain flours like rice, barley, millet, oat or wheat.

"Place two tablespoons flour in the top of a double-boiler. Add one-half to one cup water or milk to the flour. Place directly over low heat and simmer until thickened, five to 10 minutes. Now place the cereal over boiling water and cook 45 minutes to one hour."

To add to the nutrition and palatability of cereal (before your baby doctor okays whole milk), mix it with breast milk or formula. As your baby's diet broadens, you can add pureed fruits, but do not sweeten with sugar or honey.

Vegetables

Whenever possible, use fresh vegetables or ones frozen without salt, sauce or seasonings. Canned foods should be avoided for baby food use because of their high salt and lead content. To feed your baby wholesome, nutritious vegetables, it is neither necessary nor advisable to pay health-food-store prices for so-called "organic" produce. "Organic" is a poorly defined and often misused term and its appearance on food labels does not guarantee that the foods are free of pesticides and other chemicals. Spot checks of such products have proved time and again that they can be as high — or higher — in pesticide residues as their supermarket counterparts. Furthermore, produce in health food stores is generally delivered less often and has a longer shelf time, so you may be getting fewer nutrients for more money.

Steaming, baking, microwaving, pressure cooking, or boiling in a small amount of liquid (also consumed) are the best cooking methods for preserving nutrients in vegetables. Scrub produce thoroughly to remove pesticides and bacteria. Many foods (including potatoes) retain nutrients better when cooked whole and unpeeled.

Cook vegetables until soft, but do not overcook. Remove skins, strings, and seeds. Remove the baby's portion and puree with some of the cooking water, breast milk, formula or milk before adding seasonings (no salt for anybody) to the remaining vegetables for the rest of the family.

Among the vegetables to avoid during the baby's first year are cucumbers, onions, cabbage, brussels sprouts, broccoli, cauliflower and turnips. They have a strong taste, are difficult to digest and produce gas. Babies should not be fed home-prepared spinach, beets, turnips, collard greens, and carrots until about nine months to one year of age (consult your doctor) because of the vegetables' naturally high nitrate levels. These nitrates may be converted in an infant's immature digestive system to nitrites. They not only may be carcinogenic, but can interfere with the oxygen-carrying capacity of the blood. Commercial foods, with the exception of beets, are not troublesome, though you may want to delay introduction of highly allergenic tomatoes and corn.

Vegetables recommended early are green beans, peas, squash, white or sweet potato and asparagus. Introduce them one by one, but don't hesitate to try new vegetables on your youngster . . . and the rest of the family. Variety is one of the keys to a good diet, so there's no point in letting your child grow up thinking — as many of our generation did — that there are only three vegetables in the world — peas, green beans and candy-coated carrots.

As your baby grows and develops, the vegetables and other foods he eats should become lumpier and more varied (your own version of junior foods). First blend or grind them to a coarser consistency, then mash or chop. If there are certain vegetables or other foods the baby refuses, don't be concerned and don't make a fuss. Babies are very versatile. Try the food again in a month or so. Similarly, foods that cause a reaction can be tested again after the first birthday.

Fruits and Juices

One of the best and easiest fresh fruits comes practically ready to serve. Babies love, and readily accept, very ripe banana that you can mash with a fork. Mix with breast milk or formula at first for a smoother, thinner consistency. Ripe avocado can also be mashed and served. Another ready-to-feed treat is the unsweetened "adult" applesauce found in glass jars in the regular food section. It's a lot less expensive than products in small jars for babies, and the rest of the family loves it, too. Canned fruits have an excellent texture for pureeing, but purchase only fruits packed in water or their own juice in cans that are not lead-soldered.

Initially, you will have to steam or stew and then puree the other fruits you serve your infant. For either cooking method, fruit should be washed, peeled and cut up. Steam or simmer fruit (about one cup fruit to ¼ cup water) about 15 minutes or until tender, then puree.

When the baby has been introduced to a variety of foods, you can begin combining fruits or blending them with cottage cheese, plain yogurt, and so on. You can also begin introducing scrapings from raw fruit, blended raw fruits (adding apple juice or water if necessary), mashed fruit, and then pieces of soft raw fruit. Berries and seedless grapes should be withheld until about the age of two.

Your baby is ready for juice when he can drink it from a cup. You may use the same juices you buy or squeeze for your family, but delay highly allergenic citrus juices until your pediatrician gives the go-ahead. Do not serve your baby fruit "drinks" or "ades," which are primarily sugar, water and artificial colors and flavors, or juices from lead-soldered cans.

Protein Foods

After your baby has been introduced to a variety of cereals, fruits and vegetables (at approximately six to eight months of age), he will be ready for more protein-rich foods, such as meat, poultry and beans. As breast milk or formula consumption begins to diminish, these foods will be an increasingly important source of iron and many B vitamins.

Meat for the baby can be cooked by virtually any method (except frying) and then pureed with cooking liquid, water, juice or milk. Cooking meat in a crock pot or pressure cooker is an ideal way to tenderize it, but you can also use meats baked, broiled or stewed for the rest of the family. If you season the adult dinner, remove your baby's portion first.

If preparing meat just for your baby, a simple method is to trim the meat into cubes removing all fat and gristle, and then bring to a boil in a saucepan with one cup of water per cup of meat. Reduce the flame and simmer until the meat is tender. Cool and then place it in the blender with one-quarter cup of stock for each cup of meat. Meat can also be put through a grinder and mixed with liquid. Freeze excess.

Favorite beginning meats for babies are beef and chicken, but you can also move on to pureed veal, lamb or pork. Full of nutrition and acceptable to most babies when prepared in the above manner are liver (chicken, calf, beef), kidney and heart. Because it is so rich in vitamins and minerals, liver is often hyped as an ideal baby food. It is an excellent source of iron, vitamins A and D, and other important micronutrients. But, as with all good things, liver can be overdone, as an overzealous mother recently learned by feeding her twins daily rations of chopped livers. Both children had serious side-effects from a vitamin A overdose. Liver is also extremely high in cholesterol. Serving it once a week is probably good nutritional insurance for the baby and parents alike, but should not be done on a daily basis. Liver and other meats may be more readily accepted by your baby when mixed with a vegetable (i.e. steaming chicken livers and carrots, and puree with cooking liquid).

A good way to prepare meat for the infant just starting is to scrape a piece of raw or lightly broiled meat with a dull knife or spoon and then cook the resulting pulp over boiling water, with milk or water added if desired. For cleanliness and low fat content, it's a good idea to puree or grind meats yourself at first; later you can move on to lean, store-ground beef. Some mothers find it handy to store single servings in small sandwich bags to be cooked as needed.

Dr. Spock suggests adding white, non-oily fish such as halibut, flounder and haddock to the baby's diet by 10 or 12 months of age. Baby's portion can be taken from what you boil, bake, broil or poach for yourself, or prepared by the meat directions mentioned earlier. Carefully remove all skin and bones before blending, crumbling the flakes between your fingers to detect even the smallest bones.

Some meats should be avoided early on because of their high levels of fat, salt and nitrates and/or nitrites. They include bacon, sausage, hot dogs, bologna, salami and other cold cuts, corned beef, ham, and sardines and other salted, smoked or processed fish.

Other high-protein, high-iron foods you can begin adding to your young one's diet are dried peas and beans cooked soft, then pureed (try limas, garbanzos, kidneys, pintos, lentils, and so on), mashed, strained, or blended with cottage cheese or unsalted tofu, and plain yogurt. One of the best foods for your baby, but a controversial one, is eggs. They are extremely rich in the iron and protein the baby needs from solid food sources, but are also highly allergenic, so many nutritionists and doctors suggest delaying their introduction.

If your family has a history of allergy, you would probably do well to hold off on serving eggs until the ninth to twelfth month; your physician may advise you to do so in any event. However, because it is the yolk that is very rich in iron and the white that causes allergic reaction, it is generally safe to introduce cooked egg yolk earlier. Start with just a fraction of a teaspoon and be alert for any reaction. You can hard-boil the egg and mash the yolk with milk or water and use the cooked white in salad or other adult foods, or separate the egg first, cook the yolk in boiling water and save the white for baking or adding to another egg to produce a lower-cholesterol adult omelet or scrambled eggs. Your baby can probably begin partaking of whole eggs — scrambled or soft-boiled — between nine and 12 months of age. Your doctor will advise you.

So much for feeding your baby soft, pureed foods — his introduction to the world of adult eating. That bright and curious little bundle isn't going to be satisfied with this semi-liquid diet for long, however. Soon he'll be craving food with some real texture, grabbing at everything in sight, and attempting to feed himself. Don't be nervous; it's the beginning of another fascinating chapter in your baby's life, one we'll deal with next.

LEAD: A HEAVY BURDEN FOR INFANTS
AND CHILDREN

Dr. Herbert Needleman, director of lead exposure studies at the Children's Hospital Center in Boston and an assistant professor at Harvard Medical School, recently conducted experiments that produced convincing evidence of a link between lead and childhood learning and behavioral problems, such as hyperactivity, impulsiveness and difficulty in following instructions.

Needleman measured the lead content of baby teeth from more than 2000 first- and second-graders and found that children with high dentine lead scored significantly lower on IQ tests than did their classmates with low lead concentrations. Moreover, the children with higher lead levels were consistently rated by their teachers as more easily distracted, less organized, and, in general, less able to function well in the classroom. None of the children in the study showed overt symptoms of lead poisoning — gastrointestinal disturbances, pallor, weakness, pain and stiffness in joints, bones and muscles, neurological and ocular disturbances, anemia, kidney damage, impaired thyroid and immune system function, and so on.

Because lead is virtually everywhere in our environment (the air, the soil, the water), it is a simple matter for the average adult to absorb 50 to 60 mcg of lead a day — the arbitrary limit above which it is believed adverse health effects are observed. But for infants and children, who absorb lead much more efficiently, and are undergoing rapid brain development, less lead can cause adverse effects. As a result, children are more likely to be harmed by lead than adults.

You have little control over your child's lead intake from some sources, but you can limit it in the food he eats. Food may account for about 55 to 85 percent of a person's daily exposure to lead. People who rely heavily on canned and processed foods are getting significantly more lead than if they ate fresh foods. Lead levels are higher in processed foods of all types. Hamburger, for example, has five times the lead of fresh beef. But lead-soldered cans are the worst culprits.

Although only about 10 to 15 percent of all food is canned, lead solder alone is responsible for 14 percent of the lead in the average American diet. Lead solder is used to seal the seams of cans, and a lead solder plug is used to seal the hole through which evaporated milk is injected into cans. Leaching of this solder into canned food can double or triple its lead content. A four-ounce serving of canned, baked beans, for example, can contain between 50 and 60 mcg of lead, and a similar serving of sauerkraut can yield 450 mcg! The estimated maximum tolerable intake of lead for infants is 50 mcg, for children 100 to 150 mcg, and for adults 250 to 400 mcg. The safe level for pregnant women is considerably lower than other adults because of possible harmful effects on the developing fetus. There are a number of ways you can reduce your family's ingestion of lead.

• Buy fresh, whole foods whenever possible; avoid processed foods.

• Do not feed infants and children food or juice from lead-soldered cans. Foods in two-piece cans (rounded bottom, no side seam) and welded cans (neat, narrow side seam colored blue-black) do not contain high amounts of lead and are safe to buy.

• If you occasionally buy foods or juice in lead-soldered cans for older family members, never store food in them once opened. That practice can increase lead levels as much as seven times. Recently, health officials in South Carolina, investigating the apparent lead poisoning of three children, found dangerous lead levels in opened cans of orange juice in their refrigerators. Just eight ounces of one of the cans contained 270 mcg of lead, and eight ounces of the other had more than 850 mcg. Both far exceeded the safe daily intake level.

• Do not store food in ceramic containers: many glazes contain lead that can be leached by food.

• Never give children bone meal supplements. Ninety percent of body lead is deposited in bone, so anybody taking large quantities of bone meal is also getting potentially harmful levels of this and other toxic metals. Cases of lead poisoning from this practice are not uncommon.

Meat Content of Baby Foods*

	% meat
Meat and broth	65
High meat dinner	30
Vegetable and meat dinner	8

*Minimum standards for fresh, uncooked meat

Source: Helen Black, editor, The Berkeley Co-op Food Book, Palo Alto, California: Bull Publishing Co.).

LEAD CONTENT IN FOODS

	Lead level in 1970s (ppm)*	Lead level in 1980 (ppm)
Evaporated milk	0.52	0.08
Infant formula	0.10	0.02
Baby food juices	0.03 (canned)	0.015 (glass)
Solid baby foods (glass)	0.15	0.03
Adult food (canned)	0.38	0.21

*parts per million

Reprinted from "Lead in Canned Foods," Robert M. Schaffner, *Food Technology* (Dec. 1981), with permission of the Institute of Food Technologists

---

Infant Heights and Weights*

Age	Sex	Usual Length Range	Usual Weight Range
6 months	Girl	24¼ in. to 27¾ in.	12 lb. 12 oz. to 19 lb. 4 oz.
6 months	Boy	25 in. to 28½ in.	13 lb. 12 oz. to 20 lb. 12 oz.
9 months	Girl	26 in. to 29½ in.	15 lb. 8 oz. 22 lb. 8 oz.
9 Months	Boy	26¾ in. to 30¼ in.	16 lb. 8 oz. to 24 lb.
1 year	Girl	27½ in. to 31¼ in.	17 lb. 4 oz. to 24 lb. 12 oz.
1 year	Boy	28¼in. to 32 in.	18 lb. 8 oz. to 26 lb. 8 oz.

Source: National Center for Health Statistics

*Approximately 90 percent of babies fall into these ranges. Greater or lesser length or weight may be normal or may indicate a nutritional or health problem. These figures should be viewed as guidelines only, not as requirements your baby should fulfill. Your doctor is the best judge of your baby's state of health and nutrition.

A CALENDAR OF BABY'S CONSUMPTION

Month	Foods	Portions
5	Breast milk or iron-fortified formula	Breast-feed 4 to 5 times a day or on demand.
	Infant cereal if advised by doctor	If bottle feeding, 6 to 8 oz., 4 to 5 times a day, at least 27 oz. total.
		If needed, start with 1 tsp. of cereal.
6	Breast milk or iron-fortified formula	Breast-feed 4 to 5 times a day or on demand.
	Cereal	If bottle feeding, 6 to 8 oz., 4 to 5 times a day, at least 30 oz. total.
	Strained vegetables and fruit	
	Can start strained meat or strained legumes (dried peas and beans)	2 to 3 tbsp. solids at each of 4 to 5 feedings.
7	Breast milk or iron-fortified formula	Breast-feed 4 to 5 times a day or on demand.
	Cereal	If bottle feeding, 6 to 8 oz., 4 to 5 times a day, for a total of 30 to 32 oz.
	Strained vegetables and fruit	
	Strained meat or legumes	6 to 7 tbsp. of various solids at each of 3 to 4 servings.
	Dry toast for teething	
8	Breast milk or iron-fortified formula	Breast-feed 3 to 4 times a day or on demand.
	Cereal	If bottle feeding, 6 to 8 oz., 3 to 4 times a day, about 30 oz.
	Finely chopped vegetables, fruit, meat, poultry, dried beans and peas, cheese	6 to 7 tbsp. of various solids at each of 3 to 4 feedings.
	Juice from a cup	
9	Breast milk or iron-fortified formula	Breast-feed 3 to 4 times a day or on demand.
	Cereal	If bottle feeding, 6 to 8 oz., 3 to 4 times a day, total intake of less than 30 oz.
	Chopped vegetables, fruit, meat, poultry, dried	

A CALENDAR OF BABY'S CONSUMPTION

Month	Foods	Portions
	beans and peas, cheese Juice from a cup Finger foods	7 to 10 tbsp. of various solids at each of 3 to 4 feedings.
10	Breast milk or iron-forti-fied formula Cereal Chopped vegetables, fruit, meat, poultry, dried beans and peas, cheese, rice, noodles, macaroni Juice from a cup Finger foods	Breast-feed 3 to 4 times a day or on demand. If bottle feeding, 3 to 4 times a day, total intake less than 30 oz. 7 to 10 tbsp. of solids at each of 3 to 4 feedings.
11	Breast milk or iron-forti-fied formula Cereal Chopped table food—vegetables, fruit, meat, poultry, dried beans and peas, cheese, rice, noo-dles, macaroni Juice from a cup Finger foods	Breast-feed 3 to 4 times a day or on demand. If bottle feeding, 3 to 4 times a day, total intake less than 30 oz. 7 to 10 tbsp. of solids at each of 3 to 4 servings.
12	Breast milk or iron-forti-fied formula Cereal Chopped table food—vegetables, fruit, meat, poultry, dried beans and peas, cheese, rice, noo-dles, macaroni, eggs Juice from a cup Finger foods	Breast-feed 3 to 4 times a day or on demand. If bottle feeding, 3 to 4 times a day, total intake less than 30 oz. 7 to 10 tbsp. of solids at each of 3 to 4 feedings.

*This is a rough guide only. The time of introduction of foods and amounts fed will depend on your infant, doctor, and so on.
Source: What Shall I Feed My Baby?, USDA Food and Nutrition Service.

MOVING UP TO LUMPS & CHUNKS

When a baby moves from liquids and strained foods to solid foods, he is usually between six and nine months old. This is a feeding milestone. It may come as the first gleaming tooth, a sip from a cup, a grab for the spoon, or your baby trying to shove everything into his mouth by hand. Your baby's menu during this formative period will have to change quickly to keep up.

Fruit, vegetable, cereal, and protein food consumption will increase and take on a wider variety and chunkier texture. Some people who feed commercial baby foods switch to the junior and toddler varieties at this time. But those foods aren't necessary because by the time the baby is ready for them he can usually handle soft-textured adult foods: mashed vegetables, hamburger and other coarsely ground meat, fish, poultry, fruits, macaroni, rice, breads, cereals, peanut butter and soft cheeses. Besides, many "junior" foods contain salt and sugar and are not a significant step up from the strained food in variety and texture. It's time your baby had a challenge.

The pediatrician may not yet have given the go-ahead on some highly allergenic and difficult-to-digest foods, but your baby's repertoire has expanded considerably. Much of what your family eats will find its way into your baby's mouth in a modified form.

The potential allergens, once approved, should be consumed in small amounts at first. Orange and other citrus juices, for example, may be diluted with water. Don't introduce such foods during bouts of diarrhea, when your baby's intestinal tract is already irritated.

Hand/eye coordination, balancing while seated, chewing (despite few, if any, teeth), and other skills are developing apace. Your baby will desire more substance to his food; you should be alert for signs that he's ready for more texture and coarseness in his foods. As Kenda and Williams aptly point out, "One advantage of making your baby's food is that you can create just the right textures for the condition of his teeth and the strength of his urge to chew." First you cease to puree foods; then you begin to blend or grind them coarsely, then grate, dice, and finally cut into small pieces with a knife. The change to mashed or chopped foods should be accomplished gradually to avoid digestive problems.

The baby food cookbooks, with their suggestions for older infants, will prove useful and inspiring. You'll also want to begin introducing and/or emphasizing the foods that play an important role in your own good diet: rice, peas and beans, vegetables of all varieties, fresh fruits, whole grain breads, cereals and pastas, low-fat yogurt, cottage and other cheeses, and fish and poultry. Your baby is probably also ready for peanut butter (mixed with a little milk at first to prevent choking) on small bits of whole grain bread.

Cup feeding of milk (when allowed), juice, water, and the like should be encouraged despite any mess that ensues, and will probably be readily grasped by your baby, who is open to and intrigued by every new experience. You'll probably find by this time that feeding is not something you do "to" your baby, but "with" him. He is probably grabbing the spoon now, and such efforts should be encouraged, no matter how primitive or ineffective. But don't push him.

The learning experience, independence, and healthy interest in food are as important as the nourishment taken in. Don't worry if more food ends up on the baby than in it. Many parents have created a "safe zone" for the baby by pulling the high chair away from the wallpaper and spreading a plastic tablecloth or shower curtain underneath it. Newspaper works great, too, and is disposable. Touching, squeezing, mashing, rubbing, and even dropping food are all part of your baby's education, so be patient, and

Kids are notoriously messy when they eat.
Some mothers like to lay down newspaper
to keep dinner off the floor.

don't be concerned about neatness; give the young adventurer plenty of meal time to explore as well as eat. And satisfy your baby's insatiable appetite for new tastes, colors, smells, shapes and textures by providing a constant parade of new or differently prepared foods.

Kenda and Williams accurately describe this creative period: "As the months go by and the teeth come in, you can make your food ever chewier and lumpier and more various, just waiting to be fingered and rubbed and spread all over your kitchen. And loved! You won't be wanting your baby to sit passively by while an insipid mixture is spooned into his mouth. The textures and smells and colors and real feels of your homemade food will have him at the top of his class in dexterity, in feeding himself, in feeling independent and accomplished and happy with the world."

Just as you shouldn't worry about the mess (food throwing should be discouraged, however), you shouldn't worry whether the baby is getting enough to eat during these creative eating sessions. Like the rest of us, babies have no desire to starve, and will manage to get more than an adequate amount from hand to mouth. When the baby has gained the independence of being a self-feeder, don't interfere by feeding him with your spoon while he is busy attempting to scoop up cooked carrots. Not only may your baby lose interest in feeding himself, you may wind up with a fat baby from force-feeding it. Likewise, before your baby picks up the spoon and you are still doing the feeding, be attentive to his desire to stop eating. Don't force food past tightly clamped lips. Your baby hasn't read the rule that says one must finish everything on the plate or in the bottom of a jar, and it's just as well. An overfed, fat baby often becomes the same kind of adult.

Once the baby is drinking milk, it should be offered at the end of a meal, not with it. Most babies love their milk and will eagerly fill up on it, leaving little room for the iron-rich foods they need at this age. The result could be a condition called "milk anemia."

One of your child's favorite activities at this time will be picking up food and attempting to transport it to the mouth, where it will be sucked, mashed, gummed, chewed, and, yes, even swallowed. Your child is entering that joyous period known as "finger foods." Says Dr. Spock, "This is good training for them as preparation for spoon-feeding themselves at about a year. If babies are never allowed to feed themselves with their fingers, they're less likely to have the ambition to try the spoon.

"By nine months you are mashing the food instead of straining it, and you can leave unmashed some of the pieces of string beans, cauliflower, avocado, asparagus, potato, yams, and carrots. Babies will want to pick up these pieces, along with particles of meat, and put them in their mouths. They can also chew on a slice of raw apple, orange or pear." Allowing children to pick up food and put it in their mouths helps them make the transition from pureed to lumpy foods. The transition is one that should begin at about nine months; if put off until one year of age, it becomes harder and feeding problems may result.

By all means, let your child attempt to eat his regular food with fingers or a spoon. You may have to share feeding chores at first. Offer a selection of fascinating finger foods that he can pick up, chew, and swallow without choking. Most of the following foods are appropriate for the majority of babies older than nine months; those that are starred may be offered even earlier. Seek the doctor's advice and don't try to exceed your baby's abilities.

Break the food into small pieces to help your baby eat.

FAVORITE FINGER FOODS

Toasted bread cut in sticks, cubes and other shapes*

Chunks of banana*

Graham crackers*

Canned fruits (water or juice packed in welded cans)*

Arrowroot cookies*

Cheerios*

Orange sections with membrane and seeds removed

Wedges of peeled apple (perhaps steamed at first) and other soft fruits (pears, peaches, plums, avocado, and so on).

Soft cheese in bite-sized cubes (American, gruyere, cream, and so on).

Cold, cooked carrot sticks (cooked vegetables are suitable for finger food when they can be pierced easily with a fork)

Tender young lima beans

Cooked broccoli and cauliflower flowerets

Chunks of cooked white or sweet potato

Chunks of cooked summer squash

Soft peas

Cooked strips of zucchini or crookneck squash

Soft, string-free green beans

Salt-free crackers

Creamy peanut butter, cheese spread, egg salad, pureed meat, and so on, on bread cubes, banana, etc.

Cooked liver (veins and membrane removed)

Fish sticks

Macaroni in a variety of shapes (whole-grain or at least enriched). Serve plain or with butter, tomato sauce or cheese

Rice

Tiny cubes of cooked, soft chicken, turkey, fish (remove all bones)

Small bits of lean, drained ground beef

Tiny meatballs

Cooked egg yolk

Thick pieces of fluffy omelet or frittata

Cubes of soft, salt-free tofu

THUMBS DOWN ON THESE FINGER FOODS

May Cause Choking

Nuts

Seeds

Raw carrots

Raw celery

Popcorn

Raisins

Olives

Snack chips, pretzels, etc.

Bread sticks

Grapes

Hard or chewy candy

Hot dogs

Whole-kernel corn

Berries

Tough or stringy meat

Dry cereal flakes

Crumbly baked goods

Too Much Fat and/or Salt

Bologna and other cold cuts

Hot dogs

Sausage

Bacon

Vienna sausage

Hard to Digest

Cucumber

Raw, leafy vegetables

Raw onion

Chocolate

Take Place of Nutritious Foods

Cookies

Cake and other desserts

Sugar-coated cereals

Candy

Snack chips

FASCINATING FINGER FOODS

Sesame Snaps

1¾ cups whole wheat flour
¼ cup sesame seeds
¼ cup vegetable oil
¼ to ½ cup water

Mix flour and sesame seeds in large bowl, stir in oil and mix well. Add just enough water to create pie dough consistency. Roll out dough to 1/3-inch thickness and cut into circles or other shapes with cookie cutters. Place on ungreased cookie sheet and bake in pre-heated 350-degree oven until crisp.

Graham Crackers

2 cups whole wheat flour
½ cup wheat bran
½ cup wheat germ
1 teaspoon low-sodium baking powder
½ teaspoon baking soda
½ cup margarine
½ cup brown sugar
½ cup milk

Stir together the dry ingredients. Cream the margarine and brown sugar until fluffy. Add flour mixture alternately with milk, mixing well after each addition. Chill dough for several hours or overnight. Preheat oven to 350 degrees. Roll dough out extremely thin directly onto greased cookie sheets, and cut into squares. Prick with fork and bake 10 to 12 minutes, until brown. Makes 24 crackers, about 2½ by 5 inches. Seal airtight to stay crisp.

(Laurel Robertson, Carol Flinders, Bronwen Godfrey, *Laurel's Kitchen,* New York: Bantam Books)

Reprinted by permission from *Laurel's Kitchen: A Handbook For Vegetarian Cookery & Nutrition,* by Laurel Robertson, Carol Flinders and Bionwen Godfrey © 1976, Nilgiri Press, Petaluma, CA 94953

Meat Sticks

1 pound lean ground beef
¼ cup wheat germ
1/8 cup bread crumbs or uncooked oatmeal
1 egg
dash garlic powder
vegetable oil

Combine all ingredients and shape into two-inch sticks. Add just
enough vegetable oil to skillet to cover bottom of pan. Brown
sticks on all sides, then add half inch of water or broth, cover and
simmer about half an hour. Drain.

Frittata

1 teaspoon vegetable oil
1 egg
1/8 to ¼ cup grated or diced zucchini or other squash
1/8 cup grated cheese (optional)

Preheat broiler to about 450 degrees. Heat oil in small, 6-inch
skillet (preferably cast iron) on top of stove. Saute squash until
just tender over medium heat. Pour beaten egg over squash and
sprinkle with cheese if desired. Let cook about 1 minute and then
place under broiler a few minutes until egg is fluffy and begins to
brown. Cool and cut into pie-shaped pieces. (For adults, increase
proportions, saute a minced clove of garlic with squash, serve
hot).

Fish Balls

1½ pounds fish fillets (halibut, etc.)
1 egg
1 onion, minced
2 Tablespoons cracker crumbs
approximately ½ cup water

Grind fish and mix with beaten egg, minced onion, cracker
crumbs and water. Form into balls and place in steamer basket
over water. Cover tightly and steam over low flame about two
hours, adding water as necessary.

TEETHING FOODS

As your baby's teeth begin to come in, he may become fussy
and irritable, cry constantly, and lose his appetite. You can
sometimes relieve pain in the gums by rubbing them with your

finger and by encouraging the baby to chew such items as fluid-filled plastic teething rings that can be frozen, or an ice cube tied inside a washcloth. Vicki Lansky also suggests trying a stale bagel, a frozen banana, or large, clean, cold raw carrot. You can, of course, buy graham crackers, teething biscuits or toast, or make your own. An easy way to harden fresh bread is to toast it at low temperature in the oven for about 20 minutes. Or try this recipe:

Teething Biscuits

2 cups whole wheat flour
1 cup sugar
2 eggs

Beat eggs thoroughly and add sugar. Stir in flour. Roll out on floured surface until 3/4 inch thick. Cut into circles or squares and place on greased cookie sheet. Let stand 10 hours and bake in pre heated 325 degree oven until brown.

MY BABY THE VEGETARIAN?

It may seem inconsistent with the diet proposed here that meat, eggs, cheeses and other high-fat foods are listed among those appropriate for your baby. With careful food choices, adults who stay on strict vegetarian diets (no animal products of any type, including dairy products and eggs) can live healthy lives. Infants and young children, however, need animal protein in order to grow and be healthy. Youngsters raised on strict vegetarian or vegan regimens whose only source of animal food is breast milk are susceptible to vitamin and mineral deficiency diseases (i.e., rickets and anemia), protein deficiency, inadequate caloric intake, malnutrition, retarded growth, even death.

On the other hand, if you follow a carefully planned lacto-ovovegetarian (includes dairy products and eggs) or lactovegetarian (includes dairy products) diet, your youngster can be raised on it from infancy with no adverse health effects. Such children grow up healthy and strong. If you want your child to be raised on veganism, such a plan should not be instituted until he is about five years of age, and then he must receive supplemental sources of vitamin B 12 (unavailable in plant foods) and calcium. Additionally, in order for your youngster to be well-nourished, his diet must be carefully selected to provide sufficient calories, a good balance of essential amino acids, and adequate sources of riboflavin, iron, and vitamins A and D. Vegetarianism is laudable, but such a plan must be implemented carefully and at the proper age.

COMPARING FAT CONTENT OF VEGETARIAN/NON-VEGETARIAN CHOICES

Food	Calories	% Calories From Fat
Ground beef, lean, cooked, 3 oz.	190	47
T-bone steak, trimmed of fat, cooked, 5.8 oz.	370	41
T-bone steak, with fat, cooked, 10.4 oz.	1400	82
Veal, loin, cooked, 4.5 oz.	300	50
Chicken, light meat, without skin, cooked, 5 oz.	230	20
Turkey, light meat, roasted, 3 oz.	150	20
Tuna, packed in water, 1/2 can	120	6
Crab, cooked, 1/3 lb.	140	18
Egg, large, boiled or poached	80	63
Milk, whole, 1 cup	160	50
Cheddar cheese, 1 oz.	110	73
Peanut butter, no fat or sugar added, 1 tbsp.	80	75
Almonds, roasted in oil, 1/2 oz.	90	78
Coconut, fresh, grated, 1/4 cup	70	86
Sunflower seeds, dry, hulled, 1/4 cup	200	75
Avocado, medium size, 1/2	140	93

Source: Adapted from *The Fat Counter Guide,* Ronald M. Deutsch, Palo Alto, California: Bull Publishing Co.

Moreover, if your incentive to vegetarianism for your child is based on health issues rather than moral, ethical or religious ones, you can, with careful selection, do as well for him with a diet that includes judicious amounts of lean meat, fish and poultry as you can with a poorly instituted lacto-ovovegetarian plan that relies heavily on high-fat cheese and cholesterol-rich eggs. As emphasized again and again, the key to a healthful low-fat diet is proper selection and preparation of foods and, above all, moderation.

Some final points to remember if you are considering a vegetarian regime for your baby:

• If your doctor withholds highly allergenic eggs and milk for the first year, your baby will need some other source of animal protein.

• High-residue (i.e., high fiber) diets, which vegetarian plans generally are, may result in intestinal irritation and/or diarrhea in an infant and may interfere with proper absorption of other nutrients. The Canadian Pediatric Society does not recommend high-residue vegetarian diets during the first two years of life.

• The diet of a lacto-ovo or lacto-vegetarian baby would have to rely heavily on milk as a source of protein and other nutrients. Cow's milk can cause small amounts of blood loss from the intestines of some babies (from sensitivity to a protein constituent of milk). The more cow's milk consumed, the more blood that may be lost. Small amounts of blood loss over several months can lead to iron-deficiency anemia.

• Babies are less likely to become sensitized to particular foods if fed moderate amounts of a wide variety rather than relying on large amounts of one or two (such as milk and eggs).

• Vegan diets do not provide adequate nutrition for infants and young children and may prove harmful or fatal. Zen macrobiotic diets are unsuitable and potentially dangerous for persons of all ages. If your convictions tell you that either kind of diet is right for you, that is one thing. But your youngster, for whom such a diet can be harmful, doesn't have the luxury of being able to make such a choice for himself.

• If you are considering a lacto-ovovegetarian diet for your baby, seek your doctor's advice regarding feeding.

TIME FOR TABLE FOOD

At about one year of age, there's nothing keeping your baby back from eating what he wants. He's ready for whole or low-fat milk (unless the doctor okayed it earlier), whole egg, any other potential allergens, plus just about anything else the rest of the family eats. Feeding is something your little one does pretty much by himself now, provided the more challenging fare is cut into small pieces. You should continue to withhold tough or stringy meats, nuts, or other foods that could induce choking. It's still important that you provide balanced nutrition, offer a broad and interesting array of foods, and create an atmosphere for developing good eating habits and a healthy attitude toward food.

BREAKFAST

Start the day with a good breakfast. By setting an example for the child, perhaps the parents won't skip this all-important meal either. No one's day should begin without breakfast, and the habit of sitting down to eat in the morning is one that must be cultivated early. Children who don't eat breakfast are faced with a number of problems, and generally grow up to be adults who skip breakfast. Most of us who eat lunch at noon are more than ready for dinner six or seven hours later, yet we blithely skip

SUGARED CEREAL SCOREBOARD

Less Than 10% Sugar	% Sugar*
Farina	0
Oatmeal	0
Puffed Rice	0
Wheatena	0
Wheat Germ	0
Puffed Wheat	1
Shredded Wheat	1
Cheerios	3
Chex (Wheat, Rice, Corn)	4
Corn Flakes	5
Kix	5
Post Toasties	5
Special K	5
Grape-Nuts	7
Rice Crispies	8
Total	8
Wheaties	8
Kellogg's Concentrate	9
Kellogg's Product 19	10

11–20% Sugar

Buc Wheat	12
40% Bran Flakes	13
Grape-Nuts Flakes	13
Team	14
Life	16
All-Bran	19

21–30% Sugar

Life, Cinnamon Flavor	21
Nabisco 100% Bran	21

SUGARED CEREAL SCOREBOARD

21–30% Sugar (*continued*)   **% Sugar***

Quaker 100% Natural 21
Frosted Mini-Wheats 26
C.W. Post 29
Raisin Bran 29
Cracklin' Bran 29

More Than 30% Sugar

Golden Grahams 30
Granola . . . . approx. 32
Cocoa Puffs 33
Trix 36
Honey Comb 37
Alpha-Bits 38
Count Chocula 40
Cap'n Crunch 40
Sugar Frosted Flakes 41
Quisp 41
Lucky Charms 42
Cap'n Crunch's Crunch Berries 43
Cocoa Krispies 43
Cocoa Pebbles 43
Fruity Pebbles 43
Cookie-Crisp 44
Frankenberry 44
Sugar Corn Pops 46
Super Sugar crisp 46
Froot Loops 48
Apple Jacks 55
Sugar Smacks 56

(Compiled from: "Sucrose and Glucose Content of Commercially Available Breakfast Cereals," *Journal of Dentistry for Children,* Sept./Oct. 1974; *Jane Brody's Nutrition Book.* NY: W.W. Norton; *Earl Mindell's Vitamin Bible For Your Kids,* NY: Bantam Books; *The Berkeley Co-Op Food Book,* Palo Alto, CA: Bull.)

breakfast and don't eat until lunch, making the elapsed time between meals as many as 18 hours. No wonder we are cranky, ravenous, and inefficient. No wonder studies show that children who miss breakfast are careless and inattentive and do poorly in school. No wonder they are more likely to fall victim to infection and fatigue.

Likewise, those who skip breakfast are more likely to snack between meals, usually on the less-than-desirable fare offered by school and office vending machines, and end up putting away more calories (empty ones at that), than those who sit down to a wholesome breakfast. Breakfast is a vital meal and an important habit to get into, yet most youngsters miss it altogether or prepare their own without parental input or supervision. That usually means having a high-sugar cereal.

Breakfast doesn't have to be an elaborate affair. Indeed, most of us would do well to bury our traditional ideas of what this meal should consist of. The usual fat-filled bacon, cholesterol-rich eggs, pancakes swimming in syrup, and candy-coated cereal can be replaced by quick, nutritious foods. To assure you have time for breakfast in the morning, get everyone up 20 minutes

These cereals are low in sugar and salt and are made from nutritious wheat and oat grains.

earlier than usual and have as much of the meal as possible prepared the night before.

Cereal is easy to prepare and a favorite. The selections *you* (not your child) make should be based on the ingredients lists, not on television commercials or cute names. Most cereals are insipid concoctions of refined grains and sugar, sugar and more sugar. Some, however, are sugar- and salt-free and provide good nutrition, plus the kind of convenience that will assure they get from cupboard to table in the morning. If you have the time and are so inclined, you can make your own low-cost hot cereals from whole grains, but that's not really necessary. Many commercial products provide comparable nutrition with a lot less hassle. Oatmeal and Wheatena are particularly good choices. Omit the salt called for in preparation. You'll be keeping sugar in the cupboard for judicious use in baking, but keep it off the table! You've worked hard to keep your child from developing a sweet tooth, so there's no reason to start now. Hot or cold, cereal can be sweetened with fresh fruit. And beware of granolas — touted as "health food" cereals; the addition of honey, molasses, dried fruits, nuts, coconut, oil, and so on, makes many of them very high in fat and more sugar-laden than some of the "junk" cereals. Nutrition and health writer Jane Brody reports using granola, "which is too high in sugar and fat to be eaten alone, for a garnish on an unsweetened whole wheat, oat, or bran cereal."

Anyone would get bored with cereal every morning, and kids are no exception. Fortunately, your choices are unlimited. You can, of course, serve the old standbys — french toast, waffles (make up extra and freeze to pop in the toaster on busy days), pancakes, and eggs. Now that your baby has joined you at the table, his consumption of eggs and other cholesterol- and fat-rich foods should be reduced, however.

But there's no law that says you have to stick to traditional "breakfast" foods. Many kids who wouldn't touch an egg in any form and balk at hot cereal, would relish a breakfast sandwich — scrambled egg with mayonnaise and mustard on whole wheat toast, grilled cheese (or quesadilla), peanut butter and banana on raisin bread, sliced turkey or chicken with lettuce and sprouts, pita bread stuffed with whatever's on hand, or even a hamburger. For an open-face sandwich, try strips of cheese melted on toast covered with tomato slices; refried beans spread on a crisp corn tortilla and sprinkled with cheese; cream cheese on a bagel; cottage cheese and cinnamon on whole-wheat bread placed briefly under the broiler. The possibilities are limitless. Remember that anything you serve at other meals is just as wholesome at breakfast. Kids love foods like cold leftover pizza (or English muffin pizzas), macaroni, last night's casserole, or even a bowl of soup or chili.

For rushed mornings you can make your own "instant" breakfasts in the blender with such ingredients as fresh fruit, juices, yogurt, wheat germ, cottage cheese, brewer's yeast, non-fat milk, an occasional raw egg, even sprouts. These make a particularly hearty breakfast when teamed with one of your nutrition-packed muffins made in advance. Fresh fruit is a good accompaniment to any morning meal, and generally has fewer calories than more concentrated juice, plus the valuable fiber. Try adding lemon juice to bananas for an interesting taste.

What you serve for breakfast is limited only by your imagination. You should all eat something. "Something," however, should not be taken to mean fat-filled, high-calorie doughnuts and other pastries. And remember that a glass of non-fat milk can give a good nutritional shot in the arm to the most haphazard meal. Other top-notch breakfast ideas can be found in *Jane Brody's Nutrition Book,* and Vicki Lansky's *Feed Me! I'm Yours* and *The Taming of the C.A.N.D.Y. Monster.* Here is a sampling of what you can do with breakfast:

TAKE A BREAK FOR BREAKFAST

Bird's Nest

1 slice whole-grain bread
1 egg
margarine

Let your child bite a hole in the center of a slice of whole-grain bread (instead, he may use a round cookie cutter). Spread margarine on both sides of the bread. Brown one side of the bread in a greased skillet, then flip over. Crack an egg into the hole in the bread, cover and cook until egg white is set. (Use fancy-shaped cookie cutters for special occasions.)

Peanut Butter and Jelly Muffins

2 cups whole wheat flour
½ cup sugar
2½ teaspoons low-sodium baking powder
¾ cup peanut butter
¾ cup non-fat milk
2 eggs
¼ cup jam or jelly

*Use chunky style or add chopped peanuts for bigger kids

Mix flour, sugar and baking powder in large bowl. Cut in peanut butter with pastry blender until mixture acquires consistency of coarse crumbs. Lighly beat eggs in separate bowl and mix in milk. Add liquid to dry ingredients and stir until just moistened. Place half of mixture in greased muffin tins. Place approximately one teaspoon of jam or jelly in each cup and top with rest of batter. Bake at 400 degrees in pre-heated oven for 15 to 17 minutes. Makes about 12 muffins.

Hearty Oatmeal

4 cups non-fat milk
2 cups oats (not instant)
½ cup raisins
1 or 2 apples, peeled and slivered
Cinnamon to taste or 1 teaspoon brown sugar or molasses
  (optional)

Mix all ingredients except cinnamon and sugar together in saucepan. Bring to a boil, reduce heat, cover and simmer, stirring often, for about 10 minutes or until oatmeal reaches desired consistency. Top with cinnamon, brown sugar or molasses, if desired. Yield: 4 servings. (A meal in a bowl.)

Reprinted from *Jane Brody's Nutrition Book* by permission of W.W. Norton & Company, Inc. Copyright © 1981 by Jane E. Brody.

Fruity, Nutty Granola

8 cups uncooked oatmeal
2 cups shredded, unsweetened coconut
1 cup wheat germ
½ cup sesame seeds
1 Tablespoon cinnamon
1½ cups chopped nuts (almonds, walnuts, peanuts, pecans,
  sunflower seeds, etc.)
1 cup chopped raisins, dates or other dried fruit
¾ cup honey
½ cup vegetable oil
2 teaspoons vanilla

Mix together first seven ingredients in large bowl. In a separate
bowl, mix together honey, oil and vanilla. Add liquid to dry ingredients and mix thoroughly. Place mixture in two 15 x 10 inch
pans and bake at 350 degrees for 30 minutes or until golden
brown. Cool, stir with fork and store in covered container.

LUNCH

If you're a "domestic engineer," work part-time or out of the
home, there won't be any problem controlling what your child
eats — or at least is *served* — for lunch. Soups, sandwiches and
salads are good choices, as are any of your nourishing leftovers.
Avoid canned kid foods as well as frozen dinners, meat pies, and
so on, all of which are full of salt, sugar, fat, and a host of other
undesirables. They're okay in a pinch, but don't let your kids live
on them.

Even toddlers can help make their own lunch sandwiches; they
particularly enjoy filling fat-free pita bread from an assortment
of small containers of nourishing tidbits (garbanzo or kidney
beans, shredded lettuce or spinach, diced cucumber, green
pepper or zucchini strips, split cherry tomatoes, leftover rice,
low-fat yogurt or cottage cheese) that you provide.

Sandwiches are a staple of children's lunches, but you don't
have to limit yourself to the peanut butter variety. Some authors
of recipe books seem to feel that a food isn't fit for a child unless

one of its ingredients is peanut butter. Peanut butter is a nutritious, protein-packed food, but it shouldn't be served every day; it is a high-calorie, high-fat food, even though the fat is of the unsaturated variety. The "old-fashioned" varieties that must be stirred and refrigerated are the best choice because the oil has not been hydrogenated to keep it from separating. Most brands contain salt, unless you buy the higher-priced salt-free variety, and some contain sugar, so check the labels. To pique your child's midday appetite, try some of these tempting alternatives to the sandwich:

- Crisp, raw vegetables with a wholesome dip
- Chilled fruit salad with a whole-grain muffin
- Whole wheat bread cut in cubes or shapes, spread with a nourishing food such as tuna, egg salad, leftover meat ground and mixed with mayonnaise, homemade cheese spread, garbanzo spread, cottage cheese or cream cheese, and decorated with raisins, sprouts, carrot curls, vegetable slices, and so on.
- An apple cored and sliced, stuffed with chicken salad.
- Hot soup and toast in cold weather, cold soup and breadsticks when it's hot.
- How about a homemade whole wheat soft pretzel with cheese spread and a glass of juice?

If your youngster is going to a baby-sitter or preschool and lunch is provided, find out what it consists of. It would be nice to know your nourishing meal program is being carried out full-time, and your youngster won't just be dining on frankfurters and fruit "drinks". If the school's food selections are not appropriate, make your youngster's lunch — if other kids bring theirs, too. Remember, it's just one meal, so letting your child (who's getting plenty of good food and nutritional instruction at home) eat with the other kids may be less harmful in the long run than making him feel like a freak.

If your sitter has just one or two young clients, it shouldn't be any problem to get him to care for your child the way you wish. Afterall, that's what you're paying for. If you're required to bring your child's lunch, remember that sandwiches aren't everything. You can send something hot in a Thermos (or to be heated by the baby-sitter), something cold in a container, plus a variety of finger foods. How about tuna, egg or chicken salad rolled up in a lettuce leaf?

For excellent brown-bagging and other lunch suggestions, refer to Lansky or Brody, or write to the U.S. Government Printing Office, Washington, D.C. 20402 and request USDA Food and Nutrition Service Program Aid No. 1290, a booklet of wholesome, easy recipes called *Eating For Better Health.*

To avoid being rushed in the morning, prepare lunch the night before. While you're at it, make one for you and your husband. Taking along something wholesome and satisfying to enjoy outdoors in nice weather can save you from the high-fat, high-calorie fare of restaurants, cafeterias, vending machines and lunch wagons. And bringing your lunch may leave enough time to spare for a long walk.

LUNCHES THEY'LL LINE UP FOR

Soft Pretzels

*A wholesome lunch or snack

1 loaf frozen whole wheat bread dough
Poppy or sesame seeds (optional)

On a floured surface, cut thawed dough the long way into eight strips. Cover and let rest 10 minutes. Roll each strip on floured surface or between floured hands until ½ inch thick and 18 inches long. Shape strips into pretzel shape and place on greased cookie sheets. Brush with lukewarm water. Sprinkle lightly with sesame or poppy seeds (optional). Let rise, uncovered, for 15 to 20 minutes in warm, draft-free place. Place a shallow pan of water on bottom shelf of oven. Preheat to 425 degrees. Bake pretzels on center shelf of oven for 18 to 20 minutes or until golden brown.

(*Eating For Better Health,* USDA Food and Nutrition Service Program Aid No. 1290).

Liver (Pretend) Pate

Wash and drain approximately one pound of chicken livers. Place livers in saucepan with enough water to just cover. Bring to a boil, reduce heat and simmer, covered, until cooked through. Mash or grind livers, add about ½ cup plain yogurt or sour cream (more or less depending on amount of livers and consistency you desire), a tablespoon or two of grated onion, if your kid doesn't object, and mix well. Spread on whole wheat, unsalted crackers. (A gold mine of vitamins and minerals.)

Chickpea Spread

1-¾ cups garbanzo beans (save liquid)
2 Tablespoons lemon juice
1 Tablespoon mayonnaise
¼ teaspoon garlic powder

Drain garbanzo beans, saving liquid. Mash and blend beans, add 1 tablespoon reserved liquid, lemon juice, mayonnaise, and garlic powder. Mix until smooth. If too thick, add more liquid. (Stuff in pita pockets or spread on bread.)

Variation: For salt-free garbanzo beans, cook from dry beans. Cover with two to three times as much water as beans, soak overnight. Add water and cook 1½ or 2 hours.

(*Eating For Better Health,* USDA Food and Nutrition Service Program Aid No. 1290).

Guacamole

2 avocados, very ripe
1-2 Tablespoons plain yogurt or sour cream (depending on consistency you desire)
¼ teaspoon garlic powder
1 Tablespoon salsa (optional)
1 Tablespoon lemon juice
½-1 tomato, finely diced
¼ cup shredded cheddar cheese

Scoop out meat of avocados and mash in a bowl. Add other ingredients and mix well. (Serve with warm corn tortillas or vegetable dippers.)

Chicken Salad

½ chicken
2 large celery stalks, chopped
¾ cup apple chunks
2 Tablespoons mayonnaise

Boil chicken in water. Simmer until tender (45 to 60 minutes). (To save broth for soup, cool, then refrigerate. Skim congealed fat off top and discard). Cool chicken, remove skin and bone, chop coarsely into ½-inch pieces. Mix in other ingredients. (Serve on bread, in a split tomato or apple, or rolled up in a lettuce leaf.)

Variation: Substitute pineapple chunks or seedless grapes for apple.

(*Eating For Better Health,* USDA Food and Nutrition Service Program Aid No. 1290).

DINNER

For the first year or two, your little one isn't going to have discriminating taste. Your chicken chasseur may be greeted with a crinkled nose, your garbanzo bean quiche with a giggle. It's wise to think of dinner not as food kids are supposed to like, but as the foods your family eats, served in smaller portions to the newcomer. It is also important to remember the toddler's limited capabilities and what is probably a decided preference for blander foods. You will, for the most part, want to serve your child your usual family foods. That way the foods *you eat* will become the foods *he likes,* and not vice versa; remember that small children don't generally go for foods that are spicy or highly seasoned.

Your youngster may be the exception, of course — the Toddling Gourmet — but some recipes may require you to back off on the seasoning until the baby is older. Don't overdo, though; you want your little one to develop a wide variety of tastes.

If you made your own baby food, your child has "grown up" on your cooking, so the switch to your more grown-up fare shouldn't be that big a change. You should expand his circle of foods as skill increases and taste matures. If your youngster sees you eating and enjoying what you serve, it will seem to him to be the most natural thing in the world. So while spaghetti, pizza, macaroni and cheese, hamburgers and the like are great, they aren't the sort of foods you have to serve every night because you now have a kid to feed. When preparing meals for the family, keep in mind the following:

• Good cooking doesn't have to be an elaborate and time-consuming chore. Families with two working parents (54 percent of women with children under 18 are employed), are often tempted to buy the quick, processed food in the store or to pick up a couple of sacks of fast food on the way home. Try to suppress that urge by preparing meals in advance, keeping the evening meal simple during the week (that's the best way to eat anyway), and by taking advantage of such time-savers as a crockpot, pressure cooker, food processor, blender, and/or microwave. Some working parents go on a cooking binge for a few hours on Saturday or Sunday afternoon, shopping for and cooking meals for a week or more using many of the same ingredients. Once you start cooking from scratch, you'll find that many foods made from scratch aren't that much more complicated than the expensive, salt- and additive-laced, processed mixes. For example, in the way of extra work, corn bread from scratch requires only that you measure your own dry ingredients, yet it tastes much better than the boxed stuff and allows you to use whole wheat flour and low-sodium baking powder, leave out the salt, and reduce the sugar). If you both work, or even if you don't, prepare the evening meal together. Rather than a chore required of one person, it can be a relaxing way to talk over your day.

• Dinner, like all your meals, should follow the principles of good nutrition discussed in Chapter 2. It ought to contain representatives of each of the four food groups and should be:

High In: vitamins and minerals, fiber, complex carbohydrates.
Low In: fat, cholesterol, calories, salt, sugar, artificial additives.

• Don't abandon easy, favorite recipes; instead, turn them into the more nutritious, low-fat, low-salt variety. To do so: 1) Use less meat in meatloaf or hamburger patties by adding oatmeal, wheat germ, grated vegetables (carrot, potato, zucchini, and so on), and onion. 2) Make vegetarian soups or make soup the day before, chill, and skim the congealed fat off the top. 3) Replace meat in spaghetti sauce with fresh mushrooms and crumbled tofu. 4) Instead of using meat, make enchiladas with beans and low-fat cottage cheese, lasagna with ricotta cheese and spinach. 5) Stir-fry a medley of vegetables with just a few ounces of meat and serve over rice. 6) Have a meal whose main dish is a big baked potato (keep calories low by topping with plain yogurt, buttermilk or lemon juice; garnish with crumbled bacon, chives, a sprinkle of parmesan cheese, etc.). 7) Bake with low-sodium baking powder and leave salt out of all your recipes. 8) If recipes call for canned vegetables, tomato products, and so on, buy the low-sodium brands.

• Offer variety . . . and plenty of new dishes.

• A suitable beverage for children at meals is milk.

• Don't use dessert as a bribe to get a child to eat dinner — you merely increase its importance in his eyes, promting him to view it as the "good stuff" to be sought after. Dessert doesn't have to be written off as nutritionless junk. You can make it a valuable part of the meal by serving fresh fruit, applesauce, baked apple, homemade frozen yogurt, plain gelatin made with fresh fruit or juice, or your own muffins, quick breads or cookies, baked with a minimum of sweetener, no salt, and fortified with whole grains, vegetables, fruits, nuts, seeds, and so on.

• Don't be too concerned about how much your child eats. After the dramatic growth of the first year, a child's appetite generally lessens considerably between ages one and three. You can't expect consistency from a child, either, where appetite is concerned. One day he will pick around and eat almost nothing and the next day pack it away like the fabled Coxey's Army. Try not to let it trouble you; it all tends to even out over a week's time and most kids put away more than adequate amounts.

DINNERS KIDS WILL DIG INTO

Vegetarian Pizza

1½ cups whole wheat flour
½ package active dry yeast

1 teaspoon sugar
1 teaspoon olive oil
¾ cup warm water
1 8-oz. can salt-free tomato sauce
Italian seasoning or oregano
Coarse-ground black pepper
4 oz. grated mozzarella cheese
4 oz. grated cheddar cheeze
1 green pepper, sliced in strips
4 green onions, cut crosswise
small can chopped or sliced ripe olives
1 cup fresh mushrooms, sliced

To make crust, dissolve yeast in warm water in large bowl. Mix in ½ cup flour, sugar and oil and stir until smooth. Add remaining flour or enough to create a soft dough. Kneed five minutes on a floured surface. Cover and let stand 15 minutes. Press out onto pizza pan or cookie sheet. Spread surface with tomato sauce to within ½ inch of edge. Sprinkle with Italian seasoning or oregano and black pepper. Arrange vegetables on top, then cover with cheeses. Bake on lower rack of pre-heated 450-degree oven for about 15 minutes or until crust browns and cheese bubbles.

(Let your child select the vegetable toppers.)

Quick Potato Soup

2 medium potatoes, peeled and diced
1 large carrot, diced
2 medium onions, sliced
3 Tablespoons margarine
2 Tablespoons chopped parsley
black pepper to taste
5 cups hot water

Add potatoes, carrot and onions to melted butter, cover and simmer until partially cooked. Stir in water, parsley and pepper, and simmer covered until potatoes are tender. Serves 4.

Taco Salad

Large tossed green salad
1-1½ cup cooked lean ground beef
½-1 cup shredded cheddar cheese
2-3 corn tortillas
French-style low-calorie salad dressing (recipe follows)

While putting together a large tossed green salad, cook and drain ground beef. Bake tortillas in 400-degree oven until crisp and crumbly (about 15-20 minutes). Crumble tortillas into bite-size pieces and add to salad along with meat and cheese. Toss with French dressing.

French-Style Low-Calorie Salad Dressing

1 cup tomato juice
2 Tablespoons lemon juice
½ teaspoon oregano
pinch of garlic powder
pinch of pepper

Put all ingredients together in a jar and shake well. Store covered in refrigerator. (No fat, and just 7 calories per 2 tablespoons.)

(Salad Dressing: *Eating For Better Health,* Program Aid No. 1290, USDA Food and Nutrition Service).

Build-Your-Own Bean Burritos

A versatile meal you can make with whatever's on hand. As you heat a can of refried beans and warm flour tortillas in foil in the oven, fill small bowls with garnishes: shredded lettuce, diced tomatoes, shredded cheese, plain yogurt, salsa, leftover rice, you name it. Provide everyone with a hot tortilla, a dollop of beans, and let them add what they like; roll and eat.

Black Bean Soup

1 16-oz. package black beans
6 cups water
2 Tablespoons margarine
1 Tablespoon vegetable oil
1 cup chopped onion

1 cup shredded carrot
1 cup chopped celery
1 cup shredded potato
1 bay leaf
1 teaspoon oregano
½ teaspoon salt (optional)
2-4 cloves garlic, minced
¼ teaspoon pepper
3 Tablespoons lemon juice

Place beans in a large pot and add water until two inches above beans. Soak 6-8 hours or overnight. Drain. Add beans and vegetable oil to 6 cups water and bring to a boil. Reduce heat, cover, and simmer 1½-2 hours. Saute onion, carrot and celery in margarine until tender but not mushy. Add sauteed vegetables and remaining ingredients (except lemon juice) to beans and stir. Cover and simmer another hour. Prior to serving, stir in lemon juice and garnish with a slice of fresh lemon, if you like. Yield: 6 servings, 1¾ cups each. (Make the night before, reheat after work . . . or cook slowly in a crockpot.)

Oven-Baked Chicken

1 fryer, cut up, skin removed
½ cup non-fat milk
2 cups (approx.) cornflakes or other crumbs (wheat germ can be added to crumbs for extra nutrition)
Garlic powder
coarse-ground black pepper

Dip chicken parts in milk, then roll in crumbs until thoroughly coated. Place on ungreased cookie sheet, sprinkle with garlic powder and pepper, and bake at 400 degrees for approximately one hour (insert fork to test for doneness). (Works great with fish, too.)

Real Corn Cornbread

1 cup whole wheat flour
1 cup cornmeal
¼ cup sugar
1 Tablespoon low-sodium baking powder
2 eggs
12-oz. can or package frozen whole kernel corn, drained
1¼ cup non-fat milk
¼ cup vegetable oil

Pre-heat oven to 425 degrees and grease a 9x9 baking pan or 12 muffin tins. Mix dry ingredients in large bowl. Beat eggs in smaller bowl and add milk, oil and corn. Add liquid to dry ingredients and mix until moistened. Pour into pan and bake 35 to 40 minutes or until golden brown. Goes great with soup, beans and chili.

No TV Dinner

1 pound lean ground beef
4-5 small potatoes
4-5 carrots
1 onion, chopped (optional)
pepper

Form hamburger into patties (the number will depend on the size servings — i.e., small for kids, slightly larger for grownups). Dice carrots and potatoes. Cut a large piece of aluminum foil for each hamburger patty. Fill each piece of foil with 1 diced potato, 1 diced carrot, 1 hamburger patty, and some diced onion, if desired. Sprinkle lightly with pepper. Fold foil tightly, sealing the edges. Cook in a 400-degree oven (on a cookie sheet, to avoid spills) for approximately 30 minutes or until vegetables are tender. Kids get a kick out of eating them right out of the foil. These freeze well, too, and are great for an emergency meal or that evening when the sitter's coming. Thaw first or allow extra time for cooking when frozen. Tastes terrific without the tube.

SNACKS *CAN* BE FOOD

Snacks are not only something everybody enjoys, but an important part of a child's nutrition. Think of your child as a compact car with a small gas tank that requires frequent filling. Because of their limited capacity at mealtime and their high energy levels, most kids need something extra during the day to keep them filled up, to fulfill their caloric requirements, and to ensure an adequate intake of essential nutrients. Indeed, the average child gets about one-fourth to one-third of his daily calories from snacks.

Snacks have come to mean a lot of things to Americans, few of them good. But there's no law that says snacks have to be nutritional nightmares; they can be a valuable contribution to a child's supply of complex carbohydrates, protein, fiber, and essential vitamins and minerals. When snacks are healthy, we'd probably all be better off cutting down the size of our meals and eating light snacks.

If your child is like most, he'll be ravenous between regularly scheduled meals and should be offered nourishing snacks that contribute a significant amount of the day's necessary nutrients. The sample menu chart in this chapter shows how snacks can become a significant part of a youngster's diet. Before moving on to recommended snacks and recipes, there are a few things to remember about snacking:

• It shouldn't become a way of life. Some people seem to always have a candy bar poised at their lips or their hands inside a bag of potato chips. Life is one big snack to be consumed at their desks, in front of the television, or in the car on the way to work. If your child is hungry between meals, let him have something nutritious, but don't use food as a constant source of entertainment, tension relief, or trauma abatement. If junior falls off his skates and skins his nose, comfort him with hugs, kisses, and a Band-Aid; don't stick a cookie or a sucker in his hand.

• Likewise, don't pull the old "I'm cold, you'd better put on a sweater" ploy. If your youngster isn't hungry and doesn't want a regularly scheduled snack or refuses one when *you think* heshould be hungry, go with his decision. Pushing extra food on your child now may lead to obesity later in life.

Be sure you keep wholesome foods stocked in your refrigerator. When junior comes searching for a snack, he'll find something good to eat.

• If your child is always full at mealtime but eager to munch between meals, cut down on or eliminate snacks. If he must have something, offer a nutritious snack like a glass of juice or a small piece of fruit.

• If your child is overweight, discourage snacks (and provide only those low in calories) and monitor his mealtime portions. Keep snack portions small for any youngster.

• Encourage your child to help with preparation of snacks. Not only will that take the job off your hands sooner, but it will help ensure that the snacks that do get prepared by kids when they're alone are up to your nutritional standards.

• Parents complain bitterly about their kids eating junk, junk, and more junk. But who buys the cookies, potato chips, ice cream and colas that line the refrigerator and pantry shelves?

Your kids can't eat things you don't have in the house. When they reach for candy, cola and chips, let them find fresh fruit, juices, whole grain crackers, popcorn and other approved snacks. If that's all that's there, they're guaranteed to eat it.

• Dental caries are more prevalent among people who eat between meals . . . particularly if snacks contain sugar. Fruits and some vegetables are high in sugar, too, but when chewed possess a natural detergent action that prevents them from sticking to the teeth. What sweets you do allow in your child's diet are better eaten at other meals. This is particularly true of dried fruits and honey, which stick to the teeth much more readily than ordinary sugar. Tooth brushing is as important after snacks as it is after meals.

• You can give kids snacks and desserts that taste good and are good for them by occasionally making your own. Baking snacks — and kids love to help — allows you to make cakes, cookies, muffins, and so on, with wholesome ingredients, to use low-sodium baking powder, eliminate salt, and to keep the sugar content low.

• Don't fall into the "health food" or "natural" snacks trap. Most of these items, like "natural" ice cream and candy bars (full of granola, carob, coconut, nuts, and so on) are higher in fat, sugar and calories than the majority of their "processed" counterparts.

• You can compete with the commercial sugar products that sell themselves on cute names like Ho-Hos, Twinkies, and so on. Just devise your own healthy snacks — or let your kids invent them from ingredients you provide — and give them catchy names. Joyce Hackett, an inventive mother, provides these examples: Walking Salad — anything healthy rolled up in a lettuce leaf, and Bugs on a Log — peanut butter and raisins on a celery stick.

• Finally, be sure that you have your own food priorities straight. Our generation tends to think of treats in terms of fat and sugar-filled goodies. That may be a difficult habit to get out of, even if you have changed your own eating habits. You don't want to be a nasty parent; you want your kids to have all the things that will make them happy. But if you've brought your youngsters up to be nutritionally aware, perhaps their idea of a treat is different from yours . . . and perhaps you can learn a thing or two if you'll only listen. To illustrate the point, here is some astute eavesdropping by Alice Secrist, mother of three, grandmother of three, whose desk is within earshot of the vending machines:

Child: — Oh, Mommy! Apples! I wanna apple.

Mommy: — What do you want, Sweetie? Mommy will buy you something.

C: — I wanna apple.

M: — Let's see. They have Doritos. Do you want some Doritos?

C: — No. I wanna apple.

M: — No candy, now. Candy's not good for you. Makes you have cavities and have to go to the dentist. Oh, they have Oreo cookies. Do you want to share some cookies with Mommy?

C: — No. I wanna apple, Right there. See?

M: — No sandwiches. You couldn't eat a whole sandwich. Besides, they've probably been there for days. Let's just get you a little snack. Or something to drink. Would you like a Coke? Can you say, "Coke?"

C: — Yeah. Coke.

M: — Okay. Mommy'll get you a Coke. Let's put the money in right here.

C: — Nooo! I wanna apple!

M: — Well, make up your mind. Do you want a Coke or an apple? You can't have both.

C: — *I wanna apple!*

M: — You'd better have a Coke. It'll take you all day to eat an apple.

C: — (Beginning to cry) Nooo . . . I wanna apple.

M: — Now listen to me. You just stop that crying right now. You want me to take you home and spank you?

C: — No. I wanna apple.

M: — Well, we haven't got time to eat right now. If you're a good boy, we'll stop and get you a Ronald McDonald hamburger on the way home. Would you like that? With some Ronald McDonald french fries (trailing away) . . . and some Ronald McDonald cookies . . . and some Ronald McDonald . . .

SNACKING SUGGESTIONS

— Cereal with non-fat milk

— Home-baked whole grain muffins, cookies or quick breads. Make with reduced sweetener, no salt and low-sodium baking powder.

— Individual pizzas. Use whole grain or sourdough English muffin or pita round spread with low-sodium tomato or pizza sauce, sprinkled with mozzarella cheese, a dash of parmesan and oregano or Italian seasoning, and topped with vegetables or lean hamburger that has been cooked and drained.

— Plain yogurt blended with fresh fruit (also good frozen)

— Celery stuffed with peanut butter, cottage cheese or cheese spread

— Carrot sticks and other raw vegetables with a healthful dip

— Unsalted, whole grain crackers with cheese

— Fresh fruit

— Glass of milk

— Fruit juice (can be mixed with Seltzer for a nutritious "soft drink")

— Frozen fruit juice on a stick

— Blender drinks

— Graham crackers

— Open-faced or half sandwich

— Snack-kebabs (provide toothpicks and tidbits such as cheese cubes, diced fruit, dried fruits, walnuts, and so on, and let your child create his own snack).

— Popcorn (after age four)

— Unsalted nuts (after age four)

— Unsalted pretzels

— Hot chocolate

— Rice cakes (available in health food stores and many grocery stores)

— A mug of soup or broth

— Quesadilla (see recipe)

— Unsalted tortilla chips with bean dip, guacamole, or mild salsa

— Raisin bread with margarine or cream cheese
— Cottage cheese and pineapple
— Frozen grapes, melon, strawberries, etc.
— Applesauce
— Carrot/raisin salad on a pineapple ring
— Frozen banana (put banana on wooden stick, roll in undiluted orange juice concentrate, roll in chopped peanuts or coconut if desired, freeze).
— Pick Me Up and Eat Me Jell-O (see recipe)
— Hardboiled or deviled egg
— Slices of leftover chicken, roast, etc.
— Tofu cubes, plain or cooked

GOOD AND EASY EATING

Tortilla Chips and Bean Dip

Make fat-free, low-sodium tortilla chips by cutting corn tortillas into wedges with kitchen scissors. Spread one layer deep on a cookie sheet and bake in 400-degree oven for 15 minutes until crisp and slightly browned. As a dip, use heated refried beans (stir in a bit of salsa, if desired), sprinkled lightly with cheddar cheese. (A protein and fiber-packed snack.)

Quesadilla

Lay a flour tortilla flat in an ungreased skillet (preferably castiron). Put thin slices of cheese on half of tortilla, fold, cover and place over moderate heat until tortilla begins to brown. Flip over and repeat on other side. Good with sliced tomatoes or salsa added. (A Mexican cheese sandwich.)

Pick Me Up and Eat Me Jell-O

3 envelopes unflavored gelatin
1 small can frozen juice (orange, apple, grape, cranberry, lemonade, etc.)
1½ cups water

While boiling water, combine thawed juice and gelatin. Add juice mixture to boiling water and stir until dissolved. Pour into 9x13 pan and refrigerate. When firm, cut into shapes with cookie cutters. Remove from pan with a spatula.

Oatmeal Muffins

¾ cup whole wheat flour
¾ cup unbleached all-purpose flour
1 cup uncooked oatmeal
1 Tablespoon low-sodium baking powder
3 Tablespoons sugar
1 egg
1 cup non-fat milk
¼ cup oil

Preheat oven to 400 degrees. Combine flours, oatmeal, baking powder and sugar. Mix well. In a separate bowl, beat egg. Add milk and oil. Stir well. Add liquid mixture to flour mixture and stir until just blended; batter should be a little lumpy. Pour into greased and floured muffin pan. Bake 15 to 20 minutes or until muffins spring back when touched. (Add raisins, nuts, etc., to batter if desired.)

(*Eating For Better Health,* USDA Food and Nutrition Service Program Aid No. 1290)

Cheese Carrot Spread

½ cup grated raw carrots
½ cup grated cheddar cheese
salad dressing or mayonnaise
pepper and lemon juice to taste

Mix together grated cheese and carrots. Add enough salad dressing or mayonnaise to moisten. Season with pepper and lemon juice. (Good on bread or crackers or as a dip.)

(Helen Black, ed., *The Berkeley Co-Op Food Book,* Palo Alto, California: Bull Publishing).

Baked Potato Chips

Scrub potatoes and slice thin. Spread slices on foil-lined or oiled cookie sheet and bake in a 400-degree oven for about 15 to 20 minutes or until crisp and golden brown. (Fat- and salt-free.)

(Reprinted from *Nutrition Action,* September 1983, which is available from the Center For Science In The Public Interest, 1755 S Street, N.W., Washington, D.C., 20009, for $20 per year.

SOFT DRINKS AS SNACKS?

There will come that dark day in your child's life when he discovers soft drinks. The longer you can delay that day the better. Parents who introduce small children to soft drinks as snacks or treats should have their heads examined; those who let youngsters routinely swill soft drinks at meals — including breakfast — should be put away. It's a matter of routine in most families, however, and usually occurs because mom and dad are addicted to the soda pop.

The average American consumes a third of a pound of sugar a day, much of it from soft drinks, whose consumption increased by 157 percent between 1960 and 1976 and has continued to climb at an alarming rate. Soft drinks contain water, sugar (seven teaspoons in a 12-ounce can), acid, a host of artificial colors, flavors and other questionable additives, and often caffeine. Moreover, some contain large amounts of sodium (which is linked to high blood pressure) and phosphorus, which can inhibit the body's ability to use calcium, a vital nutrient that's usually in short supply in the average diet. Soft drinks contribute nothing to a diet, except 150 empty calories and the potential to contribute to tooth decay, obesity, hypoglycemia and diabetes (in susceptible individuals), and other problems. (Fruit "drinks" and Kool-Aid are even worse, with as many as 12 teaspoons of sugar per 12 ounces!) One 1973 study conducted at the School of Dental Medicine at Tufts University showed that children who consumed just one soft drink a day for three years had 50 to 150 percent more decay in certain teeth than another group who drank water, and a higher rate of decay in all teeth. Children's teeth are much more important than money, but consider this: more than

$14 billion is spent in the United States each year to treat dental caries (cavities) and periodontal disease, ranking them among the most expensive of bacterial infections.

You may think saccharin-laced soft drinks are the answer. The Delaney Clause of the Food, Drug and Cosmetic Act suggests otherwise. The act requires banning any additive that "is found to induce cancer when ingested by man or animal." Yet the public, which is always accusing the country's legislators of letting the food industry wantonly poison us with additives, clamored to keep saccharin, their lifeline to sweetness without calories, on the market when a ban was threatened in 1977.

Saccharin has been shown to cause cancer in rats, and a National Cancer Institute study of bladder cancer patients showed they were much more likely to be heavy users (16 ounces or more of diet beverages a day) than a control group of the same age and sex without cancer. Three-quarters of the more than seven million pounds of saccharin consumed by Americans is contained in soft drinks. More than a third of all children in the United States are regular users of this sweetener and the majority of the rest is consumed by women of childbearing age; yet these are precisely the two groups most susceptible to its harmful effects.

And is the risk worth it? Consider the overweight families you frequently see in the grocery store pushing a cart overflowing with six-packs or two-liter jugs of soft drinks — usually diet soft drinks. Consider all the overweight people you've seen washing down a big slab of cake or pie with a cup of saccharin-sweetened coffee. Then consider the comments of nutrition writer Jane Brody and Dr. Michael F. Jacobson of the Center For Science In The Public Interest.

Brody: Eighty percent of the nation's 10 million diabetics reportedly use some artificially sweetened drinks and foods. But *not one study has shown that artificial sweeteners actually help diabetics control their blood sugar or that they help dieters shed excess pounds.* If anything, while saccharin's popularity soared, Americans got heavier! In fact, there is some evidence that saccharin stimulates the appetite and interferes with blood-sugar regulation, suggesting that it may be counter-productive in weight control and diabetes."

Jacobson: "The average dieter, as opposed to the strongest-willed dieter, does not automatically lose weight by eating artificially sweetened foods. The calories one avoids by drinking a bottle of diet soda are usually made up later in some other food."

So what does your child get when you serve him an artificially sweetened soft drink in place of a regular one? No sugar, no cavities, no calories. But he also takes a big risk and possibly gains a false sense of "diet security" that tells him he can eat whatever else he pleases as long as it's washed down with calorie-free pop.

In a few years you won't be able to control what your child drinks at school, on the way home from school, or anywhere else. But right now you can, and perhaps by doing so you can make a lasting impression about what's good and what isn't. Milk, unsweetened juice and water, are the recommended beverages.

YOUR CHILD WON'T EAT VEGETABLES?

Don't make a big deal about vegetables and they won't stand out in your child's mind as different and something to be shunned. But kids are unpredictable, so here are some pointers to help you cope if your youngster turns out not to like the color green.

• Don't turn your child's refusal to eat vegetables into an international incident. Your youngster will survive, and probably change his mind soon anyway.

• "Hide" grated vegetables in other foods: soups, spaghetti sauce, meat loaf, quick breads (i.e., zucchini, carrots) and the like. Vicki Lansky suggests mashing any leftover vegetable, mixing it with an egg and cooking like a pancake or baking in a muffin tin.

• If your youngster is against specific vegetables, serve him only the ones he will eat.

• Don't nag, coax or force your child to eat greens. You may be winning the battle now, but instilling a lifelong dislike.

• Prepare vegetables in a new way (i.e., stir frying) or combine with favorite ingredients. For example, a salad few children can resist is grated carrots and raisins tossed with a bit of mayonnaise.

• Serve vegetables raw with dips (see lunch recipes). Most children can't resist this method of eating.

• Let your child help shop for and prepare vegetables and salads.

• Offer vegetable slices and curls, cherry tomatoes, sprouts, and so on, to fill pita pockets or to decorate a "face" sandwich (an English muffin or cut-out slice of bread spread with cottage cheese or other filling).

• Try a tasty, low-fat sauce like "mock hollandaise" — plain yogurt flavored with fresh lemon and a dab of honey.

• Fill in with foods rich in comparable nutrients: fruits, whole grains, and legumes (baked beans, chili, etc.).

• Use vegetable cooking water to cook rice and macaroni.

YOUR CHILD WON'T DRINK MILK?

A surprising number of children, as many as 70 to 80 percent of non-Caucasians, are allergic to milk or have lactose intolerance. This inability to digest milk sugar may cause abdominal pain, diarrhea, gas, nausea and bloating when milk is consumed. Some babies cannot consume milk or dairy products in any form or quantity; others may be unaffected by moderate amounts of milk and capable of handling such foods as cheese and yogurt.

If your child has lactose intolerance, consult your pediatrician. You may need to modify your child's diet and add a calcium supplement; dairy products are the only excellent source of this vital and difficult-to-get nutrient. You'll also have to read labels carefully to assure you buy milk-free products, and cook without dairy ingredients. Vicki Lansky's *The Taming of the C.A.N.D.Y. Monster* offers excellent suggestions for coping with a milk-intolerant child, as does Jacqueline Hostage's *Living Without Milk* and *Good Eating For The Milk-Sensitive Person,* a booklet available from Ross Laboratories.

Your child may be totally unaffected by milk but refuse to drink it out of dislike. If so, you will have to use a lot of extra ingenuity to get the equivalent of the one-and-a-half to two pints of milk a day your child needs in his diet. Here are some suggestions:

• The disinterest in or dislike for milk may be temporary; don't make it permanent by nagging or wheedling.

• Many kids who won't drink milk alone will have it on cereal. If your youngster falls into that category, serve cereal often for breakfast or snacks. You can also substitute milk for water when cooking hot cereals.

• Serve dishes with milk as an ingredient: mashed potatoes, scalloped potatoes, creamed soups, vegetables with cream sauce, macaroni and cheese, puddings and so on. (Note: non-fat milk rather than whole milk or cream can be used in all of these applications.) Milk can also be used in place of water when cooking rice. Mix non-fat dry milk in with baked goods, casseroles, meatloaf and so on.

• Serve your child shakes or blender drinks made with regular or dry non-fat milk. Most kids can't resist these treats.

• Serve other dairy products: yogurt, ice milk, natural cheeses (more minerals than processed), cottage cheese. Most of these provide less calcium than milk, but are far better sources than most other foods and certainly better than nothing.

• Make sure your child's diet has an abundance of other calcium-containing foods: tofu, green vegetables, dried beans, sunflower seeds, peanuts, soybeans, sardines and canned salmon.

• And, of course, the age-old answer: Stir in a bit of chocolate or other flavoring, if your child will accept milk that way.

DOES BABY NEED VITAMINS?

Once upon a time the National Academy of Sciences made a pronouncement to all the people of America that cruciferous (broccoli, cauliflower, cabbage, brussels sprouts) and carotene-rich vegetables (carrots, sweet potatoes, winter squash, etc.) could help prevent that evil disease called cancer. The people, being very concerned about their health, decided they'd better play it safe and include those good vegetables in their diet. So they went to the grocery store, wheeled their carts quickly past the produce section, and bought bottles of "Daily Greens," a magic formula prepared by a wizard called PharmTech. Each of these miraculous and wonderful pills, costing 25 cents apiece, was the nutritional equivalent of just half a brussels sprout. But the people of the land loved the pills because they were so quick and painless and saved lots of time-consuming shopping, cooking and chewing.

If only this silly but true little fable didn't so accurately sum up the prevailing attitude toward nutrition. Americans have been having a passionate love affair with vitamins for some time now, and little wonder. Do you eat too many processed foods and get too great a share of your daily calories from soft drinks and sweets? Smoke or drink heavily? Thumb your nose at exercise? Fortunately, many of the vitamin purveyors tell us, there is no need to change any of these habits. Just relax, take a pill — better yet, take several — and you will be fit and healthy. The message has paid off, at least for the vitamin industry. We annually spend more than $1.6 billion on vitamin supplements alone, and much more on worthless foods (like heavily sugared, refined cereals) that manufacturers have tried to legitimize by doctoring them with vitamins.

When it comes to your own child, do you want him to pick up the harmful message that taking a handful of pills or a cute-shaped, candied vitamin is easier and more efficient than eating a good diet? Or do you want to spend your share of that $1.6 billion to supply your family with a variety of fresh, whole foods easily supplying everyone's daily vitamin needs, and other necessary nutrients. Unless your child has a special health or diet problem for which your doctor prescribes supplements, he should get all the vitamins he needs from wholesome foods.

WHAT ABOUT ADDITIVES?

It's breakfast time. Do you know what your child is eating? You may think you know, but you don't. The average American eats 150 pounds of some 2800 different food additives every year. Sugar and other sweeteners account for most of it — 130 pounds; salt another 15; the other five to 10 pounds consists of an assortment of emulsifiers, thickeners, bleaching agents, preservatives, flavors, colors, vitamins, and on and on.

Some food additives are useful, protecting our food supply from harmful organisms and unnecessary waste, but others are frivolous, designed to add taste and appearance to processed-to-death non-foods in order to appeal to Americans' never-ending demand for novelty. With ongoing use, some food chemicals have proved safe, but others have been consigned — sometimes too late — to the additives scrap heap. The danger with additives is that their effects may not show up for as many as 40 years, or it may be difficult to pin down an adverse reaction to a single substance. Moreover, most additives are poorly tested, particularly in the combinations we eat them. Usually the tests look only for tumors and ignore a host of other potential problems — allergic reaction, for example.

The list of ills attributed to food additives is long and diverse, but perhaps of most interest to parents is the alleged ability to cause hyperactivity and behavioral and learning problems. Implicated in particular are artificial colors and flavors, as well as caffeine and sugar. Members of the Feingold Association, named after pediatric allergist Dr. Ben Feingold (who theorized the link between hyperactivity and diet) are so convinced of the effects of food additives on behavior that they have adopted an additive-free diet for their children. Although the Feingold diet is controversial (some see a danger in communicating to a child that his behavior is based on what he eats, or attribute results to all the attention the child is getting), the program has received "tepid endorsement" from the National Institutes of Health and unqualified endorsement from 20,000 Feingold families across the country who swear by its results.

If your youngster is hyperactive or additives are of major concern to you, you may wish to learn more about the Feingold Association. Write to P.O. Box 18116, Washington, D.C. 20021. *The Feingold Cookbook For Hyperactive Children* by Ben and Helene Feingold is also available from the Association or in bookstores. If used, however, many of its recipes should have less salt and fat.

Whether or not you decide a Feingold-style diet is right for your little one, additives are a legitimate concern. Americans have the distinction of being the first people in the world to consume processed foods as more than 50 percent of their diet. And an interesting fact has developed in the past decade of "new foods.'' Almost 21 percent more Americans have cancer today than in 1971 and nearly three out of every 100 children are born with serious birth defects. Moreover, the United States has the highest number of hyperactive and learning disabled children in the world, according to Alexander Schauss, author of *Diet, Crime and Delinquency*. It isn't known how many of these ills

Additive	Where Commonly Found	Reason to Avoid
Propyl gallate	Vegetable oil, meat products, etc.	May cause cancer
Sulfiting agents	Fresh fruits and vegetables, etc.	Can cause severe, sometimes fatal, allergic reaction.
BHA	Cereals, vegetable oils, potato chips, chewing gum, etc.	May cause cancer
BHT	Cereals, oils, potato chips, chewing gum, etc.	May cause cancer
Sodium nitrite	Bacon, ham, hot dogs, lunch meats, corned beef, smoked fish, etc.	Known carcinogen in animals
Saccharin	Diet drinks and foods	May cause cancer
Caffeine	Coffee, tea, soft drinks, chocolate, over-the-counter drugs, etc.	Stimulant; causes insomnia and behavioral changes in children and some adults; possible cause of miscarriage, birth defects, fibrocystic breast disease, etc. Implicated in heart disease.
Quinine	Tonic water, quinine water, bitter lemon	Reported dizziness, etc. May cause birth defects.
MSG	Widespread in foods as flavor enhancer—soups, stews, sauces, seasonings, etc. Prevalent in Oriental cooking. (Because of public pressure, no longer used in baby foods).	Shown to destroy brain cells in infant mice. In adults, can cause burning sensation in back of neck and forearms, headache, tightness in chest.

can be attributed to food chemicals, but a host of problems are being linked to flaws in our diet and to such widely used additives as sugar, salt and caffeine. With time and improved testing methods, we'll learn a great deal more about chemicals in our food, vindicating the safe ones and banishing others. In the meantime, there are some things you can do to minimize the effects of additives on your family's health.

Although there are many questionable additives on the market, the Center For Science In The Public Interest has designated the following as the "ten least wanted additives":

• The best way to avoid additives is to buy fresh, whole foods. Frozen foods (plain vegetables, fruits, juices — not frozen convenience foods) are also preferable to canned, packaged or powdered items.

• Avoid soft drinks, sweets, junk foods, highly processed convenience foods, and diet foods and beverages. Most contribute little or nothing nutritionally, promote obesity and tooth decay, and are rife with sugar, salt, saccharin, colors, flavors and other additives.

• Eat a varied diet. Repetitious eating habits — a fast-food burger and soft drink for lunch every day, a frozen TV dinner every night — can lead to higher levels of certain additives and even greater risk.

• Don't think you can avoid additives by buying foods that tout themselves as natural. Many additives are natural substances that have proven harmful. Ironically, many synthetic additives have proven safe.

• Read labels carefully to be sure you aren't getting chemicals you've decided aren't worth the risk.

• Become better informed. Some excellent literature on the subject of food additives is available. The following are recommended: "Chemical Cuisine" poster, Center For Science In The Public Interest, 1755 S. Street NW, Washington, D.C. 20009. Michael F. Jacobson, Eater's Digest: *The Consumer's Factbook of Food Additives,* (Garden City, NY: Anchor Books). Also available from CSPI. *Eating Clean,* Center for Study of Responsive Law, P.O. Box 19367, Washington, D.C. 20036.

PARENTS NEED RULES, TOO

Nutrition educator Mary T. Goodwin has said, "Children acquire personal taste the same way they learn how to crawl, walk, or talk — through imitation, practice, encouragement and guidance." Children are never too young to begin picking up good — and bad — habits, so some rules are in order for parents at the dinner table.

Even if your baby isn't old enough to understand your words (Often something along the lines of "Yuck, spinach, let's feed it to the dog"), he can tell a lot from your attitude and your gestures. You've got to set a good example. If father makes a face when he drinks milk or mother won't touch anything green, your baby may end up not liking these foods either. Remember, you're trying to raise a versatile, healthy eater; doing so may require broadening your own diet a bit. At any rate, don't be the type of parents who loudly voice food dislikes and then wonder why the baby is a picky eater.

• In the early years, introduce new foods one at a time, not so much because of potential allergic reaction, but to avoid overwhelming a youngster whose world is constantly full of new things. Make no mention of or fuss over the new food, and introduce it in a small portion along with familiar, well-liked foods.

• If a child samples a new food, praise him. But don't complain about foods that are rejected; it merely reinforces the negative reaction. Try again later on. Kids have likes and dislikes just like adults. But what's rejected today may be relished tomorrow. Besides, there are thousands of wholesome foods out there; it's possible to lead a healthy, fulfilled life without bulgur or brussels sprouts.

• Prepare foods — particularly difficult ones — in tempting ways. It's hard to get excited over slimy, boiled okra, but there aren't many who can turn down okra when it's coated with cornmeal and lightly fried.

• Emotional blackmail has no place at the dinner table. Your child should never be led to believe that your love will be given or withheld depending on whether he eats your braised spinach. According to a newsletter from BEANS (Better Educational and Nutritional Standards), a special interest group of the California

Reading Association, "One out of five children in the United States is overweight. The cause may be the emotional overlay of food. If a caregiver offers food as a token of love, then a child may feel guilty about refusing seconds. Dr. James Corner, professor of child psychiatry at Yale University, points out children also can learn to turn to food as a comfort when they're lonely or frustrated." Likewise, babies and young children should not be induced to eat with such incentives as "Just one more spoonful for Mommy," or "Come on and eat everything up and show Daddy what a big boy you are." Your boy or girl may end up "bigger" than you'd hoped.

• Along the same lines, never use foods, especially sweets, as a reward or punishment. Some studies have shown this approach may create strong likes or dislikes. You may be creating far bigger problems than you solve. Find other ways to discipline and to reward. Contrary to popular belief, rewards don't have to be tangibles (goodies, gifts, money). Your praise and attention are much better incentives to positive behavior.

• Meals are no time to discuss that broken vase, a child's shortcomings or adult problems, airing your own arguments, or playing "Pick on Mom" as in *Diary Of A Mad Housewife* — a game children will readily fall into. Even a very young child can sense tension and strife at the dinner table. Family meals should be a pleasant time that children look forward to.

• Give your child plenty of time to eat. Feeding usually takes longer than for an adult because your child still needs time to examine and experiment with new or newly prepared foods. Allow him to eat in a calm, relaxed atmosphere so he doesn't develop the distinctly American habit of nervously wolfing down a meal. As James L. Hymes, Jr., professor of education and past president of the National Association for Nursery Education says, "Don't feel you have to hurry your child through a meal. Don't worry too much about his dawdling. Let him play with the food a little. Let him spill it, if he must. Let him use his hands if he wants to. Keep in mind your two big aims: You want him to like to eat and you want him to like to do things himself. You can't achieve either if you hurry." Perhaps in the process you'll develop a slow eater who knows he's full before he can eat enough to become fat.

• Never nag, cajole or force a child to eat; he may be full. Having the sense to stop when sated (even with food still on the plate) is a valuable attribute — encourage it.

• Don't let your child become a "food bigot." People may tell you hamburgers and hot dogs are the only foods kids like, but that's usually because it's the only food they've been fed. Introduce your child to a broad variety of foods, including ethnic dishes. The world is full of adults who refuse to try anything new or unusual and proudly refer to themselves as "meat and potato men." If you want your youngster to be open-minded about food, you've got to broaden his horizons now.

• When hands are small, even something like setting down a glass of milk is a challenge. Accidents happen, and *most* of them aren't on purpose. Kids shouldn't be yelled at or sent away from the table for such occurrences (though intentional throwing of food should be vigorously discouraged). A child who's constantly nervous about the reaction he'll get is an accident looking for a place to happen. And despite evidence to the contrary, sarcasm isn't lost on kids, either. One former child reports living in terror at the dinner table where each meal was begun with the invitation to "Go ahead and spill your milk so we can eat."

• Table manners? You say you want your child to have them? That probably puts you in the minority today, but it is a noble intention. You can look into the future a bit to see if you will get your wish by examining your own table habits today. As Dr. Spock says, kids "have a passion to copy everything they see done around them . . . Three-quarters of the things that we think we must impose on children as unpleasant duties are things they enjoy learning to do themselves at a certain stage of their development, if we only give them a chance."

There's no need to create tension at the table by nagging your child, who may not yet be physically capable of some of the things you expect from adults. Set a good example. If you sit with your elbows on the table, lick your knife, and belch your approval after each bite, you can't blame a child who follows your lead.

• Minimize distractions and don't let your young one eat meals in front of the TV. Remember that if he can't, you can't very well either. Meals should be a learning experience, a pleasant time together, entertainment in themselves. Many obese Americans who go into behavior-modification programs find that they were eating without thinking while staring at the TV. Once they begin paying attention to the meal they find they are less likely to continue eating without thinking.

The same is true of snacks. Television time (and the amount you allow is important, too), should be strictly television time, not snack time.

• You don't have to break out the fancy flatware or the damask tablecloth, but do provide an attractive and relaxing setting for meals. Kids appreciate special touches (flowers, candles, a colorful tablecloth, placemats, etc.) as much as adults do, and such touches help to make meals a positive experience.

• Serve a child small, unintimidating portions. If your child is still hungry and not overweight, he can ask for or you can offer seconds. But don't push him.

• For a very young child, use a child-sized plate with high edges, a cup with a handle he can hold easily and a child-size spoon and fork. When he expresses a desire to use the same utensils as the rest of the family, don't discourage it.

• Provide a variety of foods at each meal — hot or cold, soft or hard. Something cold, something crisp, something chewy, something colorful, and so on.

• Before long, your child will express a desire to serve himself, and you should go along with it. You can hold serving bowls or platters while he takes what he wants. You may even provide a small pitcher so he may pour milk.

• Be sure your toddler gets plenty of exercise.

• As soon as he shows an interest, let your child — male or female — participate in food selection and preparation. A BEANS newsletter describes one creative game of "going to a grocery or produce market and telling your child that he may choose five fruits and vegetables to buy and take home to eat. The child can hold the money, pay the cashier, carry the bag home, and enjoy his choices." An extension of this activity suggests you give your child a head of lettuce and a big pot of water. "Ask him to peel, tear and wash the lettuce (and eat as much as he wants!). It's a great way to develop a salad eater and a helper in your kitchen." As your child grows, he can help with the more

At this age, spoon-feeding becomes a challenge as to how much gets in the mouth and how much on the face.

complicated steps in food preparation. He'll learn valuable skills, become more independent and learn to eat wholesome foods he has had a hand in preparing. There are any number of ways you can help your child learn about food.

— A trip to the supermarket can be a valuable experience, beginning at the age a child starts to talk. As you wheel your offspring around in the grocery cart, name the foods as you put them in the cart. Let the baby hold and handle some of the non-breakables.

— Once your youngster is walking, he'll probably try to fill the cart with sugared cereals and snack chips. So give him shopping assignments. In the cereal aisle, ask him to pick up a carton of oatmeal and put it in the cart, and explain why you made that selection over the colorful cereal boxes with the sugary contents. Sidestep the candy aisle, but seek his advice on whether you should buy raisins or dried apricots for the healthful muffins the two of you will make when you get home. When kids clamor for sweet treats, offer alternatives. "No, you may not have a candy bar, but you can pick out a carton of yogurt." Better yet, make it clear before you go shopping that you won't be buying anything extra; then stick to your word.

— Teach your children about food and nutrition. Contrary to popular belief, your children will think you're the smartest person in the world, at least until they're teen-agers. If you practice good nutrition, tell them why. They'll be interested in knowing where foods come from, how grain goes from the field to the bread on the table, and so on. They'll believe you when you say that milk has calcium that makes their bones strong. And don't be surprised to overhear them telling their friends, "Some sugar is okay, but we don't like to eat a lot because it's bad for your teeth and your body." Explaining *why* your family eats certain foods and doesn't eat others is much more effective than, "Because I said so." Children are fast and eager learners; they'll readily absorb the nutritional information you provide. Just be sure you have your facts straight, and make your explanations more sophisticated as your youngster matures.

— Look through cookbooks or magazines with your child and let him help you plan meals. Start with a salad and go on to vegetables, the main dish and dessert. Asking, "What would you like for dinner?" is too vague and leaves room for stock answers like "hot dogs" or macaroni and cheese. By offering a couple of choices, you can sneak in new and nutritious dishes you want to serve, and your child has a vested interest in the meal because he chose it.

— If you have the space, plant a small garden and get your children involved. Home-grown vegetables are difficult to resist. If you don't have a garden, let him sprout beans and seeds to be used on salad, sandwiches and soups.

Many children's books — both fiction and non-fiction — offer sensible information about food. Add these to the list of books you read regularly to your child. A comprehensive listing of food books can be found in *Creative Food Experiences For Children,*

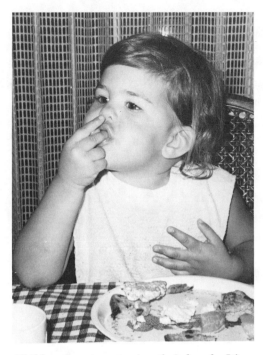

Children love to eat using their hands. It's a challenge to get the hand to the mouth.

by Mary T. Goodwin and Gerry Pollen, available from the Center For Science In The Public Interest, 1755 S. St., NW, Washington, D.C. 20009. *Creative Food Experiences* is a veritable treasure trove of effective learning experiences involving food, healthy recipes children can prepare themselves, ideas for snacks and lunches, and much more. When your child's reading skills are sufficiently developed, supply him with cookbooks geared toward children.

With your youngster around, dinner isn't going to be the quiet, romantic affair it once was. In place of the linen and candles, you are likely to have a milk-soaked Snoopy tablecloth. Instead of engaging in sparkling repartee with a nattily dressed dining companion, you will probably be asked the same question 32 times by someone with mashed potatoes in his eyebrows. You'll need your patience and sense of humor at dinner.

WHY TEACH YOUR CHILD TO COOK?

- Children are more likely to eat what they helped prepare
- Promotes independence and self-confidence
- Provides you with a good helper in the kitchen, someone who can assist with meal preparation and put together his own healthy snacks
- Improves math and reading skills
- Provides a useful activity you can perform as a family
- Provides an arena for conveying nutritional information
- Produces healthy, independent adults who learned disease-fighting cooking the painless way and aren't helplessly dependent on convenience foods and restaurant meals

RECOMMENDED DAILY DIETARY ALLOWANCES FOR INFANTS AND CHILDREN

Age (years)	Weight (kg)	(lb)	Height (cm)	(in)	Protein (grams)	Vit. A (mcg RE)
0-0.5	6	13	60	24	kg×2.2	420
0.5-1	9	20	71	28	kg×2.0	400
1-3	13	29	90	35	23	400
4-6	20	44	112	44	30	500

Age (years)	Vit. B_6 (mg)	Folacin (mcg)	Vit. B_{12} (mcg)	Calcium (mg)	Phosphorus (mg)
0-0.5	0.3	30	0.5	360	240
0.5-1	0.6	45	1.5	540	360
1-3	0.9	100	2.0	800	800
4-6	1.3	200	2.5	800	800

Share your cooking with your child. He'll learn about food and how much fun it can be to prepare.

RECOMMENDED DAILY DIETARY ALLOWANCES FOR INFANTS AND CHILDREN *(continued)*

Vit. D (mcg)	Vit. E (mg)	Vit. C (mg)	Thiamin (mg)	Riboflavin (mg)	Niacin (mg)
10	3	35	0.3	0.4	6
10	4	35	0.5	0.6	8
10	5	45	0.7	0.8	9
10	6	45	0.9	1.0	11

Magnesium (mg)	Iron (mg)	Zinc (mg)	Iodine (mcg)
50	10	3	40
70	15	5	50
150	15	10	70
200	10	10	90

Source: Recommended Dietary Allowances, Food and Nutrition Board, National Research Council, 1980.

SMALL FRY SAMPLE MENU

AGE	BREAKFAST	SNACK
1 Year	1 cup milk 1/4 cup hot cereal 1/2 small banana	1/4 cup orange juice 1 hard-boiled egg 1 graham cracker
2-3 Years	1/2 cup milk small orange 1/2 cup dry cereal	1/2 cup apple juice cheese cubes
4-5 Years	3/4 cup milk 1 scrambled egg 1 slice toast 1/2 cup orange juice	1/2 cup pineapple juice 3-4 crackers

KID-SIZED SERVINGS

AGE	BREADS, CEREALS AND GRAINS	FRUITS AND VEGETABLES
Number of Servings	4	3
1 Year	1/2 slice bread, etc. 1/4 cup pasta 1/4 cup rice 1/4 cup cooked cereal 1/3 cup dry cereal	1/4 cup juice 1 small fruit 2 tbsp. cooked vegetables
2-3 Years	1 slice bread, etc. 1/3 cup pasta 1/3 cup rice 1/3 cup cooked cereal 1/2 cup dry cereal	1/2 cup juice 1 small fruit 1/4 cup cooked vegetables 1/2 cup raw vegetables
4-5 Years	1 slice bread, etc. 1/2 cup pasta 1/2 cup rice 1/2 cup cooked cereal 3/4 cup dry cereal	1/2 cup juice 1 small fruit 1/4 cup cooked vegetables 1/2 cup raw vegetables

SMALL FRY SAMPLE MENU *(continued)*

LUNCH	SNACK	DINNER
1/2 cup milk 1/2 peanut butter sandwich 2 tbsp. peas 1/2 peach	1/2 cup milk 1/4 cup dry cereal	1/2 cup milk 1 chicken leg 1/4 cup rice 2 tbsp. carrots 1/4 cup applesauce
1/2 cup milk 1/2 cup soup 1 slice bread apple slices	1/2 cup yoguurt 3-4 crackers	1/2 cup milk 2 oz. hamburger patty 1/3 cup noodles 1/4 cup broccoli 1/2 cup lettuce salad
3/4cup milk 1 tuna sandwich 3-4 carrot sticks	3/4 cup milk peanut butter and celery	3/4 cup milk 3/4 cup chili 1/2 cup spinach salad 1 piece cornbread

(*Source:* Adapted from *What To Feed a Child 1 to 5 Years,* Safeway's Nutrition Awareness Program.)

KID-SIZED SERVINGS *(continued)*

AGE	MILK AND DAIRY PRODUCTS	PROTEIN FOODS
Number of Servings	4	3
1 Year	1/2 cup yogurt 3/4 oz. cheese	1/2 cup cooked beans 1 oz. poultry, fish, meat 2 tbsp. peanut butter 1 egg
2-3 Years	1/2-3/4 cup milk, yogurt 3/4-1 oz. cheese	1/2 cup cooked beans 1 oz. poultry, fish, meat 2 tbsp. peanut butter 1 egg
4-5 Years	3/4 cup milk, yogurt 3/4 oz. cheese	1/2-3/4 cup cooked beans 1-2 oz. poultry, fish, meat 2-4 tbsp. peanut butter 1 egg

*Including one rich in vitamin C and one dark green or yellow.
(*Source:* Adapted from *What To Feed a Child 1 to 5 Years,* Safeway's Nutrition Awareness Program.)

HIGH-CALCIUM FOODS

100+ mg	150+ mg	200+ mg	250+ mg
1 cup cooked farina	1 med. stalk broccoli	1 oz. cheddar cheese	1 oz. Swiss or Parmesan cheese
3 oz. canned herring*	1 cup ice cream**	1 cup cottage cheese	1 cup cooked collards
1 cup cooked kale	1 cup cooked mustard greens	1 cup oysters	4 oz. self-rising flour*
1 tbsp. blackstrap molasses	1 cup cooked spinach	1 cup cooked rhubarb	1 cup milk
1 cup cooked soybeans	3 oz. pink, canned salmon*		3 oz. sardines*
5 tbsp. maple syrup**			1 cup cooked turnip greens

Source: American Academy of Pediatrics
*Very high in sodium
**Very high in sugar

FEEDING A SICK CHILD

A child who is getting a balanced diet, plenty of rest and lots of exercise is likely to be sick less often than one who has a poor diet, inadequate rest and little exercise. But an occasional cold, flu, sore throat, upset stomach or childhood illness is inevitable, particularly when your young one ventures out into the world and is exposed to other children. Fortunately, these ailments are minor and can be treated with rest and a temporary change in diet.

If the child is your first, you will probably find yourself dialing the doctor at every cough or unusual cry. Experience and your pediatrician's advice will help you determine situations that require medical attention and ones that can be weathered with home remedies. If the illness is unfamiliar and you are not certain what to do, by all means call the doctor. A careful description of symptoms (and a temperature reading) over the phone is often enough for the doctor to decide if the child should be seen or can be safely treated at home.

If the doctor prescribes medication, discuss its importance matter-of-factly with your child if old enough, and administer the

167

medicine without disguise. For infants and children who refuse medications, liquid medicine may have to be mixed in with something the child drinks. Health writers Jacqueline Seaver and June V. Schwartz, M.D., recommend not putting it "in milk, orange juice, or anything else your child is accustomed to drinking. The taste of the medicine may turn your youngster against such liquids for a long time. If it happens with a new drink or one that is not important in the child's diet, it won't matter." Tablets may have to be crushed and mixed in with something tasty.

A loss of appetite is not unusual during illness. Normal meal plans will probably go out the window and you'll no doubt find yourself grateful if your youngster will eat anything, including snack foods you don't normally encourage. Although the food you serve may change (frozen orange juice on a stick in place of a tuna sandwich, carrot curls and milk for lunch) somewhat, most of the same nutritious foods regularly eaten are appropriate during illness, but in forms more appealing to the sick child. Here are some feeding tips for minor ailments.

Diarrhea. Frequent watery stools, which can lead to dehydration, may call for temporary curtailment of milk and perhaps orange juice. Often a clear liquid diet is in order: carbonated beverages (without caffeine or saccharin), homemade soda using apple or other juice mixed with mineral water, Seltzer or salt-free club soda, weak tea, water, apple, cranberry, grape juice, tomato juice, strained lemonade, orange and other citrus juices (if tolerated), plain gelatin, and unsalted homemade broth. Popular, refreshing and nutritious favorites are homemade fruit juice popsicles or snow cones made by pouring thawed, undiluted juice concentrate over crushed ice. To give the irritated digestive tract a rest, limit the intake of solid food; bland foods like toast, crackers, mashed potatoes, rice cereal and perhaps banana and applesauce are recommended.

Sore Throat. Depending on your child's preference, try warm, soothing liquids such as weak tea, broth, clear or creamed soups, or hot cocoa (if your child is not bothered by mucus). For something different, try hot lemonade with a floating lemon slice, hot apple juice with a cinnamon stir, or cold foods and liquids such as frozen yogurt, ice cream or ice milk, homemade shakes and blender drinks, fruit slush (undiluted fruit juice concentrate mixed with shaved ice), or any of the other clear liquids mentioned here.

Constipation. If your youngster is constipated (abnormally hard or infrequent stools that may cause pain and/or bleeding), don't use laxatives or enemas unless prescribed by the doctor. If the doctor approves, try one tablespoon of corn syrup to eight ounces of formula or water in an infant's bottle to loosen the stool. For older kids, plenty of liquids, fruits, vegetables and whole grains are in order. Try adding bran to cereals and other foods and offer dried fruits as they are or stewed.

Vomiting. Withhold liquids for about an hour and then offer small amounts (an ounce or so) at frequent intervals. To limit intake at first, you can allow the child to suck on an ice cube or crushed ice. Add clear liquids gradually. Once liquids stay down, wait several hours and slowly add bland solids such as toast and crackers.

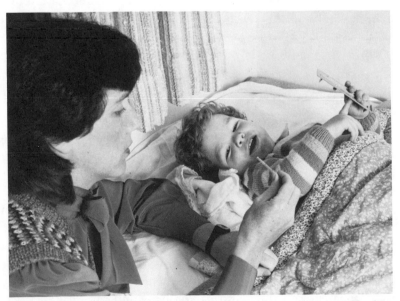

If your child is down with a cold, get out the thermometer, and let him get plenty of rest and hot soup.

Cough. In place of expensive, ineffective over-the-counter cough remedies that can cause side effects, the American Academy of Pediatrics recommends you substitute your own concoction of two parts honey, one part lemon juice and a dash of whiskey. Do not administer this formula to a child under one year of age. Warm liquids are also soothing.

Fever. With fever, as with diarrhea and vomiting, increased liquids are a must. Provide plenty of water and fruit juice, but don't force liquids.

Colds and Childhood Illnesses. If your child is feeling sick for a week or two, he may have a dull appetite. Be sure he gets some nourishment. Don't nag or waste your breath explaining how important it is to eat. Instead, try adding extra nutrition to foods the child will accept (yogurt or brewer's yeast blended with juice); offer light but wholesome foods (cottage cheese with pineapple, frozen yogurt), or make everyday foods more interesting. For example, add alphabet macaroni to broth or cut toast or sandwiches with assorted cookie cutters. If the child is confined to the house, but not to bed, his participation in food preparation may help pique interest in eating.

When your child is sick, remember the following:

- Check with the doctor if the illness warrants.
- Eliminate or offer foods as advised by the doctor.
- Offer extra liquids, especially water.
- Offer small amounts of food and drink made as attractive and appealing as possible, but don't persist if they aren't accepted. Increase interest by providing unusual eating utensils (toothpicks, chopsticks, a mug for soup, a muffin tin full of tidbits, a new "character" plate or bowl), a novelty straw, or an unusual place to eat.
- No harm will come from a break in the routine of a well-balanced diet. Don't try to force food on a sick child or nag or cajole him to eat. Forcing down food when it is unappealing may cause or intensify nausea and/or vomiting and can create a long-lasting disdain for particular foods or for eating in general.

• If your child should have a serious or prolonged illness or an illness (such as diabetes or allergy) that requires a special diet, your doctor will, of course, advise you. Keep the child from feeling deprived or different. Excellent information on special diets (liquid, soft, low-residue, high-fiber, lactose- or gluten-restricted), is available in the following publication:

Diet and Nutrition
National Cancer Institute
National Institutes of Health
Bethesda, MD 20205

HOUSEHOLD ITEMS TO AVOID

As new parents you've probably heard it a thousand times: Keep all medications, poisons, cleaning products, paints and thinners, laundry aids and cosmetics locked away out of reach.

Remember:

• High places aren't necessarily "safe" places once baby learns to climb.

• Use child-proof safety latches on all cupboards.

• Store poisonous substances in safely locked places.

• Child-proof caps on medicines and toxic products are a must. Deaths from poisoning of children one to four years of age have been reduced almost 75 percent because of safety packaging and educational campaigns. According to Seaver and Schwartz, "In those cases where a child has been poisoned by a medication, it is usually because an open medicine bottle has been left where the child could reach it." Do not foil the safety seals on products or leave the caps ajar for easy access. Store all medicines in a safe place.

• Watch your child closely in the homes of friends and family who may not be used to taking the day-to-day precautions of living with a little one.

• Do not use weed killers, insecticides or other poisons in areas where small children play.

• Do not tell your child medicine is candy or provide "candy" vitamins (some are 60 percent sugar) in cute shapes. Iron poisoning from such vitamins is not uncommon.

• Post the telephone numbers of your local poison control center and an ambulance service.

SICK DAY SPECIALTIES
(*Tasty Anytime*)

Apricot Pineapple Nog

1 cup cold pineapple juice, unsweetened
2 heaping Tablespoons dried apricots
1 egg (optional)
½ banana (optional)
3 ice cubes

Blend all ingredients until ice disappears and drink is foamy.
(Dr. Lendon Smith, *Foods For Healthy Kids,* New York: Berkley Books)

Yogurt Pops

1 quart plain yogurt
1 12 oz. can frozen juice (undiluted) or 4 cups fresh fruit (bananas, blueberries, strawberries, etc.).
1 Tablespoon vanilla

Whip all ingredients in blender. Freeze in cups, ice cube trays or popsicle molds.

Easy Eggnog

1 egg
1 cup non-fat milk
1 Tablespoon honey
grated nutmeg or a dash of vanilla

Add honey to milk in a saucepan and heat almost to boiling. Beat egg well and add very slowly to hot milk mixture, beating constantly. Remove from heat immediately and cool. Add dash of vanilla or nutmeg if desired. Serve warm or chilled.

Molasses Rice Pudding

⅓ cup brown rice
2 cups low-fat milk
2 egg yolks
2 Tablespoons molasses
¾ cup chopped dates
2 egg whites
1 Tablespoon sugar

Cook rice and milk in double boiler until tender (about 1 hour and 15 minutes). Pour over beaten egg yolks. Return to double-boiler and add molasses, dates, salt. Cook two minutes. Beat egg whites stiff; add sugar gradually. Fold into rice mixture. Chill. Serves 4.

(Adapted from Mary T. Goodwin and Gerry Pollen, *Creative Food Experiences For Children,* Washington, D.C.: Center For Science In The Public Interest)

Edible Animals

Let yours and your child's imaginations be your guide. Start with a bed of lettuce, then place half a fruit, flat side down on top. Use fresh or canned peaches, pears, apples, oranges, etc. Now decorate it to look like a mouse, spider, monster, what have you, using toothpicks to attach assorted parts. Try raisins, cherries, cloves and such for eyes and noses, circles cut from cheese or whole-wheat bread for ears, carrot curls for tails or antennae. A great way to get good things down a small sick person.

Chunky Chicken Soup

3 quarts water
1 whole chicken
2-4 cloves garlic, minced
1 or 2 tomatoes, chopped
3 stalks celery with leaves, chopped coarsely
4 carrots, cut crosswise
2 medium onions, chopped
½ green pepper, chopped
½ cup fresh parsley, chopped coarsely
¼ teaspoon crushed red pepper
¼ teaspoon tarragon leaves
Ground black pepper to taste

Place chicken (including neck, liver, etc.) in large soup pot with water and garlic. Simmer until chicken separates easily from bones (about 1-1½ hours). Remove chicken from broth, drain and cool. Add all other ingredients (noodles, rice or matzo balls) to broth. Cut chicken meat into small chunks (discard skin, bones, liver, etc.) and return meat to broth. Simmer soup until vegetables are tender. Cool and refrigerate. Skin congealed fat off surface before heating and serving.

Cottage Cheese Cinnamon Toast

4 slices whole grain bread (cut out with cookie cutters, if desired)
1 cup low-fat cottage cheese
Cinnamon

Toast bread. Spread ¼ cup cottage cheese on toast. Sprinkle lightly with cinnamon. If desired, place cottage cheese toast under broiler until cheese is warm.
(*Eating For Better Health,* USDA Food And Nutrition Service, Program Aid No. 1290)

Fruit Sherbert

¾ cup canned fruit packed in own juice (peaches, pears, apricots, etc.)
1½ cups buttermilk
1 Tablespoon fresh lemon or lime juice
Grated rind from whole lemon or lime
2 egg whites
3½ Tablespoons honey

Mix fruit andhoney in blender. Add juice, rind and buttermilk, and blend again. Pour into shallow pan and freeze until firm. When mixture is firm, mix it well and fold in stiffly beaten egg whites. Freeze one to two hours.

Fruit And Juice Gelatin

1 Tablespoon unflavored gelatin
2 cups unsweetened fruit juice (do not use fresh or frozen pineapple juice; it will not gel)
1 cup sliced fruit such as peaches, pears, apples, bananas, berries, etc.

Mix together ¼ cup juice and gelatin in a bowl. Measure another ¼ cup juice, boil it, then add hot juice to the above mixture and stir until gelatin is dissolved. Add remaining juice and stir. Put in refrigerator to set. After the gelatin begins to set a little, add the sliced fruit and return gelatin to refrigerator until firm.

(*Eating For Better Health,* USDA Food And Nutrition Service, Program Aid No. 1290)

Sunny Citrus Cooler

1 cup fresh or fresh frozen fruit (strawberries, blueberries, etc.)
Juice of one lemon or lime
Juice of two oranges
1 banana
1 cup cracked ice

Mix ingredients in blender.

AN UPHILL BATTLE

Keeping your youngster on the right nutritional track isn't going to be an easy task. He's going to be affected by a wide variety of outside influences. It's the parents' responsibility to keep a reign over their childrens' eating habits. Be prepared for the following influences:

TELEVISION

The passion most kids develop for junk foods comes from someplace, and quite often it's the TV set. As the American Academy of Pediatrics points out, there are more than 92 million television sets in the United States — twice as many televisions as children! Children in this country manage to watch one of those sets on the average of three to five hours a day. In a year of television watching, most children see more than 20,000 commercials, two-thirds or more for cereal, candy and toys. Not only can television warp your child's view of violence, love and sex, it can prevent him from participating in other activities necessary for optimal physical and mental growth (i.e., exercise, reading, social interaction, etc.), and severely distort his attitudes about how he ought to eat.

Reading to your youngsters is a pleasant diversion from watching television.

Watching television with your children gives you a chance to choose the best programs.

Children are much more susceptible than adults to the powers of advertising, but the program can be as big an influence as the commercials. Recent studies have noted the prevalence of food and drink (most of it snack foods, soft drinks and alcohol) and references to them in television programming. The message to kids, say experts, is that people on television, few of whom are overweight, can eat junk foods and guzzle beverages with no adverse health effects. Indeed, they are slim, healthy, famous, and rich! According to Michael Morgan of the University of Pennsylvania's Annenberg School of Communications, the unhealthy messages we get from programming are even more powerful than from commercials. Because commercials are more explicit, viewers may tune them out, but with programming, according to Morgan, "You're not even at that level of defense. Programming's hidden messages have a much steadier, absolutely invisible influence."

Equally alarming, television is second only to physicians as the American public's source of health information. Surveys show that adults who watch more than four hours of television a day generally know little about nutrition and eat poorly.

In a sobering report entitled *Edible TV: Your Child and Food Commercials,* prepared by the Council on Children, Media and Merchandising for the Senate Select Committee on Nutrition and Human Needs, Senators George McGovern and Charles Percy make these interesting points:

"Increasingly, research confirms the notion that food advertising implants food consumption values in children. One recent study, for example, found a correlation between a child's attentiveness to television commercials and the food choices he makes at the supermarket. Studies also indicate the vast majority of mothers yield to their children's food requests. There is little doubt today that advertising, particularly television advertising, affects the food preferences of children and the choices of their parents as well.

"The pattern of current television food advertising, therefore, is disturbing. A report prepared for the Ninth International Congress of Nutrition in 1972 suggests that more than 50 percent of the money spent on television food advertising may be negatively related to health."

Okay, so television is hazardous to your child's health; now what do you do about it?

• First, limit television viewing time — for yourself and your youngster. Encourage and share with your child other activities like sports, games, reading, conversation, hobbies and household chores.

• Restrict viewing, as much as possible, to commercial-free public broadcasting.

• Watch the shows you approve with your child and discuss what you have seen — the commercials as well as the programming. Be critical of junk food commercials and reiterate your own views on good nutrition. You should be at least as much of an authority in the home as that piece of electronic furniture.

• Make your views known — both positive and negative — to the TV networks and the sponsors.

• Don't succumb to the advertised junk yourself. Keep it out of the house and don't let your child pressure you into it at the supermarket.

• Get together with the parents of your child's friends and talk to them about setting similar rules about TV watching.

• For further help, contact your local PTA or Action For Children's Television, 46 Austin St., Newtonville, MA 02160. And for additional useful advice, the following are recommended: *Television and the Family,* American Academy of Pediatrics, 1801 Hinman Ave., Evanston, IL 60204. *Edible TV: Your Child and Food Commercials,* Senate Select Committee on Nutrition and Human Needs, Superintendent of Documents, U.S. Government Printing Office, Washington, D.C. 20402. *Jane Brody's Nutrition Book,* NY: W.W. Norton.

EATING OUT

Standard restaurant fare is high in calories, fat, sugar and salt. One of the best steps you can take for your family's health is to limit eating away from home. Fast-food outlets — which are taking an increasingly large bite out of the American food dollar — usually give you fewer nutritious alternatives than regular restaurants.

If the convenience of a fast-food restaurant appeals to you, the best food selection would be either the salad bar with minimal dressing or a small hamburger. Typically, a small fast-food

Most restaurants provide infant chairs for your baby.

burger (without cheese) has about nine grams of fat. The large specialty burgers have between 21 and 32 grams. Don't order deep-fried foods and don't add salt at the table.

Milk is the appropriate drink for kids, and some fast-food restaurants now serve the low-fat variety. Be sure a day's fast-food meal is balanced with two other high-fiber, high-carbohy-drate meals at home. For tips, consult *The Fast Food Diet* by Judith S. Stern and R.V. Denenberg.

FAT AND SODIUM CONTENT OF SOME FAST FOODS

Food	% calories from fat	Sodium, mg
Super burgers	50-60	700-1080
Pizza, 2 slices	30-40	800-1400
Fried chicken dinner	48-53	1915-2285
Fish sandwich	50	420-835
Taco	51-60	80-460
Milk shake	22-26	250-300

Source: Judith S. Stern and R.V. Denenberg, *The Fast Food Diet,* NY: Prentice-Hall.

In full-service restaurants, children can have a hand in deciding what they want. Discuss the virtues and vices of the various choices. If good nutrition is a habit in your family, your child's choices will probably be good ones, but remember that as a parent you do have veto rights. And there's no sense letting your child develop the opinion so many Americans have that eating out means pigging out.

If you know your young one can't eat a $6 fruit salad, try to order a child's portion. Or order the adult size and share it. Kids' eyes often are bigger than their stomachs or they want a whole order themselves, whether they can eat it or not. That's where you can exercise your right to say no. Ordering food you know a child can't eat is expensive, immoral, and encourages you to polish off the leftovers so they "don't go to waste." Ask the waiter to put the order on two separate plates in the kitchen, if need be.

Children's plates are usually economical and there is generally at least one suitable choice. But if they include nothing but cleverly titled hot dogs and peanut butter and jelly sandwiches, go for something else. A cup of soup (though it's probably inordinately salty), a slice of bread and a small dinner salad can be a nourishing and inexpensive meal for a youngster. Order dressing on the side so it can be applied judiciously.

Chicken, fish, veal and lean beef are good choices, as long as they are baked, broiled, roasted or grilled rather than fried. Ask for rice or a baked potato in place of french fries and order vegetables steamed, without sauce.

In more casual restaurants and coffee shops, good choices for a youngster are a hamburger without the fat-filled "secret sauce," a sandwich on whole wheat, sourdough or rye bread, pasta, chili, pizza without high-fat meat toppings, a bean burrito or tostada, and Oriental dishes. Request that no soy sauce or MSG be added. Your child doesn't have to get stuck in the traditional "kid food" rut, however, and should be encouraged to sample a wide variety of foods, as long as they are low in fat and sodium. Avoid foods that are fried, drenched in butter, a fattening sauce, or swimming in gravy. Milk is the drink of choice for children, unless it's a special occasion you think calls for a soft drink or "Shirley Temple."

If your family dines out only occasionally, you can afford to be a little less strict about what your child chooses. But if your family eats a large number of meals away from home, you've got to be careful about your choices.

BABY-SITTERS

Because no one can be a parent 24 hours a day, your child's nourishment will occasionally be left in the hands of a baby-sitter or other non-family member.

The best way to be sure that a baby-sitter will feed your child appropriately is to minimize choice. When the sitter comes to your house, leave a prepared dish he can heat or serve cold. You'll have a nutritious meal for your child, and the sitter won't be too busy cooking to keep an eye on the child. Make sure the dish you leave is one of your child's favorites; the baby-sitter has enough to do without trying to get your youngster to eat something he hates.

If there are restrictions on what you want your child eating while you're out, tell the sitter. The sitter won't know cookies and potato chips are off limits unless you make it clear. Better yet, provide nutritious snacks. If you have important instructions — feeding or otherwise — leave them in writing.

If your youngster will be going to a sitter's house while you work, select a sitter whose views on nutrition fall into line with yours. If that's impossible, at least try to get the sitter to make some concessions: milk in place of fruit drinks, a piece of fruit in place of dessert, and so on.

RELATIVES

Grandparents, aunts and uncles, and other relatives and friends can be your best allies if you make sure they show their love for your child through ways other than rewarding him with sweets. Explain the negative nutritional characteristics of sweets to your relatives. If grandmother wants to bake goodies now and then, ask her to use whole grains and to reduce the sweet ingredients. Why not give her a couple of low-sugar muffin or cookie recipes? If friends and relatives want to bring treats when they come or provide them when your youngster visits, help them out by giving them a list of approved foods. Possibilities are fresh fruit, carrot sticks and other fresh vegetables, unsweetened fruit juice, unsalted nuts, popcorn, and so on.

Treats don't have to be food, nor do they have to be expensive. Kids always appreciate balloons, stickers, dime store toys, small writing tablets, homemade bean bags, books, and scores of other cheap treats. If all else fails, order your child a "Please, No Junk Food" T-shirt from the Center For Science In The Public Interest, 1755 S. St., NW, Washington, D.C. 20009, and let him wear it when he goes calling.

HOLIDAYS

You can let down your hair a little on holidays, but they can still be occasions to celebrate good nutrition. Most of us do more baking for holidays, but you can be sure your homemade goodies are wholesome food by making them low in salt and sugar and high in whole grains and other nourishing ingredients. How about whole grain gingerbread Santas for Christmas, a low-fat, low-sugar carrot cake for a birthday, and colored popcorn for Halloween?

Christmas stockings, Easter baskets, Halloween bags and party nut cups don't have to be filled with candy; children also appreciate fruits, nuts, crayons, individual bags of popcorn, toy jewelry, and the inexpensive favors available for these holidays. Follow the lead of one enterprising mother who made her 15-month-old an Easter basket of plastic, pull-apart eggs filled with goldfish crackers and Cheerios. Instead of dragging home a bag of sweets on Halloween, why not take your youngster somewhere that evening, or become involved in a worthy cause.

For simple, festive ideas for holiday fare and favors, the following are highly recommended:

— Vicki Lansky, *Feed Me! I'm Yours*

— Mary T. Goodwin and Gerry Pollen, *Creative Food Experiences For Children,* Washington, D.C., by Center For Science In The Public Interest

— Helen Black, ed., *The Berkeley Co-Op Food Book*

— *The Feingold Handbook,* Feingold Association of the United States, Drawer A-G, Holtsville, NY 11742

A LOW FOOD BUDGET

Chances are your bosses didn't give you raises just for having a baby, so now you're trying to feed three as cheaply as two. Healthwise, maybe that isn't a bad idea. The sorry state of the American diet has a lot to do with affluence. As opposed to less fortunate people in many other countries, too many of us can afford to buy foods that are bad for us. Although there's certainly no need to quit your job in order to eat healthfully, there's no reason to think that a low food budget has to be a deterrent to good diet.

Processed foods and foods of animal origin are the most expensive you can buy. They account for the major chunk of the average American's food budget. Happily, because of their high saturated fat, cholesterol, salt and sugar content, they are the same foods you would do well to avoid. Do your wallet, your waist and your entire family's health a favor by cutting down on meat, cheese and other animal foods. When you do buy meat, buy less,and select cheaper grades just as tender and delicious with slightly longer cooking, but with less fat. Load up instead on vegetables, legumes and whole grains. Save yourself a lot of money, plus avoiding sugar, salt, fat and additives by eliminating processed foods such as boxed mixes, frozen dinners and vegetables with sauces, canned foods, processed meats, packaged sweets, snack foods and so on. And cut down on cost and undesirable chemicals by limiting consumption of soft drinks, coffee and alcohol.

There's no doubt you can eat more healthfully and save a lot of money by buying alternative protein sources and fresh, whole foods, cooking from scratch whenever possible and reducing portion size. But remember, too, a food budget that is too low can be as bad for your child as one too high. If you are unable to supply your child with an adequate diet, you should apply for assistance from the Food Stamp program through your local Social Services Department, or WIC (Special Supplemental Food Program For Women, Infants and Children), which provides food subsidies for low-income pregnant and nursing women and young children.

EATING DISORDERS

There has been a lot of talk in this book about obesity and how your child can avoid it, but there is an equally disturbing eating disorder at the opposite end of the spectrum called anorexia nervosa. Anorexia's victims — 95 percent female — are dangerously underweight rather than overweight. They have unrealistic attitudes about eating. Just as obesity is on the rise in the United States, the number of victims anorexia nervosa claims each year is increasing.

You've probably read about anorexia's terrible symptoms and puzzled over why attractive, intelligent young girls could do such a thing to themselves by refusing to eat. The descriptions of the many similarities among the families of anorexics should not be ignored. Although the cause of anorexia nervosa and related eating disorders (bulimia, bulimarexia) — which will affect one out of 100 women at some time in their life — is not entirely clear, studies reveal some remarkable similarities in home life. According to Estelle Miller, M.S.W., vice-president of the American Anorexia Nervosa Association, in 90 percent of the cases handled by the AANA, one parent in the family is an obsessive weight watcher. The parent is often preoccupied with weight, beauty and physical attributes and is usually a conscientious, educated perfectionist and high achiever. There is usually a great deal of pressure to succeed.

The onset of the disease can often be traced back to a chance remark about baby fat or teasing about "plumpness" that is the result of a girl's natural development. A girl or boy may be encouraged to lose a few pounds by a parent, a peer, a dance teacher or a coach who doesn't suspect or isn't concerned about the course the weight loss will take.

Nearly all researchers blame to some degree the equation of thinness with beauty in societies such as ours. Perhaps, too, the problem is compounded by the media and advertising we are continually exposed to. Christopher Athas of the National Association of Anorexia Nervosa and Associated Disorders points to the popular women's magazines as an example. They give recipes for tempting, calorie-rich desserts on one page and the latest fad diet on the next. Television commercials are the consummate artists at convincing us — with the help of emaciated actresses — to want what we're constantly told we shouldn't have. Perhaps an eating disorder is the ideal way of not having your cake and eating it too.

Everywhere we turn — magazines, newspapers, movies, television — we see that the heroines, the chosen ones who model the skin-tight jeans and the new fashions, are slim and svelte. They are beautiful, admired, and — the implication is clear — loved. Potentially anorexic girls, says Dr. Jean Rubel, president of Anorexia Nervosa and Related Eating disorders, "feel that if they become beautiful — defined by our society as thin — people will love, protect and revere them. They lose weight and it doesn't happen, so they lose more weight instead of revising their erroneous thinking."

Such an overriding passion to please is by no means new behavior to the anorexic. As the title of a fictionalized account of an anorexic by psychologist Steven Levenkron points out, she is quite often *The Best Little Girl In The World*. Dr. Rubel characterizes the anorexic before the onset of the disease as "caught in a conflict between perfectionistic behavior and powerful feelings of not being good enough. She is good, bright, cheerful, compliant, eager to please, cooperative, helpful, the teacher's pet, her parents' delight, and too good to be true." Eventually, however, "She gets tired of being compliant and rebels in a passive way: She stops eating."

Continues Rubel, "Before the condition appears, anorexics tend to be obedient, cooperative, outgoing and charming children who aim for perfection in everything they do. They do not rebel as overtly and energetically as other adolescents do when they reach the teen-age years and begin to separate from the parents. The parents are usually proud of their outstanding child and do not realize this goodness is not natural or healthy. Parents of anorexics have been described as overprotective, overconcerned, and overambitious. Eventually the anorexic comes to refuse everything — including food — the parents and the world have to offer. They would rather starve than continue to comply and accommodate."

In today's uncertain world, there are no guarantees against eating disorders, but a lot of parents would do well to change some of their own bizarre behavior:

• Realistically assess your attitudes about your own body. Are you really overweight? If not, for heaven's sake stop talking about it. How can a child develop realistic attitudes about body image when a normal or underweight parent is constantly talking about his latest diet or how fat he feels? If you are overweight, stop talking about it and do something about it. Get off the yo-yo diet (stuff one month, starve the next) once and for all by doing something effective for a change. Adopt a sensible, moderate, lifelong diet and exercise plan that will take weight off slowly and keep it off.

• Don't let diet — even good diet — become an obsession. Keep food and talk of food in its place. It is the staff of life, not the *purpose* of life. You should be involved in — and encourage your child in — a world of other interests.

• Don't dwell on it, but provide your child with a nutritious, balanced diet that isn't full of empty calories to make him overweight without providing all the nutrients he needs.

• Don't put pressure on your child to be perfect and always succeed.

• Don't tease a child about his weight.

• Don't use food as punishment or reward and don't offer rewards or incentives for weight loss. Your child may become too successful at this game.

• Finally, consider this reply from Dr. Rubel to the question of how parents can stop eating disorders before they start:

"About preventing eating disorders in the first place: My position is that both anorexia and bulimia are learned behaviors and coping devices used by individuals who have not acquired more mature, effective survival skills. For example, the woman who feels she has no power or control over any other area of her life may focus all her energy and power strivings on her body and try to control that, thinking if she does, she then is doing something important and significant in this world.

"Traditionally, little boys are socialized to explore their environments, to go out into the world to learn and conquer. Little girls, on the other hand, are more sheltered and protected, and in the process they are prevented from developing some of the coping strategies boys acquire. When the little girl hits a rough spot (the death of a loved one, leaving for college, the demands of career politics, marriage), she has no repertoire of survival skills to fall back on, because she has always depended on someone else to look out for her, and at that point she may fall into the trap of simplistically thinking she can fix whatever is wrong or painful in her life by making her body conform to the models in fashion magazines or actresses on television. After all, don't these women, the thin ones, have it all? Aren't they loved, respected, admired, and don't they solve all their problems in 30 minutes minus time out for commercials?

"I believe parents can help their children, especially their girls, avoid the pitfalls of eating disorders (and alcoholism, drug addiction, etc.) by allowing them to develop as wide a range of coping skills as possible. The problem is, of course, well-meaning parents do not want to watch their kids stub their toes, fall down, get skinned knees and elbows, before they learn to walk. Too often, conscientious parents prevent their children from learning life's hard lessons by protecting them and making everything too easy. Kids need to make mistakes and learn from those mistakes. In this way they build self-confidence and a sense of power and mastery. People with high self-esteem and a knowledge of their own power and mastery tend not to be the people who develop anorexia and bulimia.

"One other item. Many of the mothers of people I see and talk with are themselves much too fascinated with a slim body image. If mother is always talking about dieting and being thinner, daughter is going to get the message that 'Being slim, slimmer, slimmest will make me desirable, but being rounded is a sign of inferiority and will make me ugly and despised by everyone.' I believe one of the best things mothers can do for their children is be effective role models of a competent, confident, self-loving woman. That is a tall order in today's world with all of its conflicts, tensions, changing role expectations, and economic, political and ecological catastrophes! I seriously wonder if any of us is capable of raising happy, able, confident, unafraid, fully functioning children in a world none of us was prepared for. I get angry at the burden so often put on mom. Some people seem to relish that suggesting eating disorders are all her fault. How can parents who were children themselves in the relatively secure and innocent 1940s and 1950s teach their kids to deal with a world that none of us suspected or anticipated?"

For more information about eating disorders, contact one of the following agencies:

Anorexia Nervosa and Related Eating Disorders, P.O. Box 5102, Eugene, OR 97405, (503) 344-1144.

American Anorexia Nervosa Association, 133 Cedar Lane, Teaneck, NJ 07666, (201) 836-1800.

National Association of Anorexia Nervosa and Associated Disorders, P.O. Box 271, Highland park, IL 60035 (Enclose self-addressed legal-size envelope with 35 cents postage).

IN CONCLUSION

Near the end of a book devoted to childhood nutrition, it may be difficult to remember there is much more to parenting than feeding a child. Eating is just a small part of life. You can't afford to spend every waking moment preparing and eating "perfect" foods and neither can your youngster. Too many Americans have become obsessed with what they eat ("Is it pure enough?" "Is it low in calories?"), leaving the door open to food quackery, eating disorders, and an unhealthy self-absorption that cuts them off from the rest of life's bountiful feast.

Your goal is not to become a "food bore," perched on the sidelines of every occasion self-righteously munching carrot sticks while the rest of the company enjoys the food, the wine, the music and the conversation. Nor is it to create a child who stands by unhappily at a birthday party while the other kids eat cake. Just remember to exercise moderation and to minimize your consumption of fat, salt and sugar on a daily basis so you can relax and enjoy the special occasions . . . as well as a longer, healthier life.

Remember, too, that you are parents and have assumed the responsibility of making important choices for your child. If you weren't vital to his growth, development, well-being, and very survival, he might just as well leave home at an early age as baby birds and kittens do. Several decades of indulgence and permissiveness have proved that kids not only need, but want, their parents' guidance, discipline, love and attention. They want them more than all the items advertised on television that mom and dad's money will buy.

Your youngster isn't going to hate you for teaching him to eat right. A good diet shouldn't be regarded as a sentence imposed upon a child, but rather as a wonderful opportunity and a sure sign he is loved. Your attitude and example are all-important. If you don't instill in your child the typically American notion that the bad stuff is better, he'll never feel deprived. Good luck — and good eating — to all of you.

POSTPARTUM: THE FOURTH TRIMESTER

T he labor and delivery of your baby is an exciting and much-awaited event. However, all too often the expectant couple considers the childbearing time as only the nine months of pregnancy before birth. The "fourth trimester," the three months following the baby's birth, is an important period in any new parent's life, and should be considered in any discussion of the mother's fitness profile.

Many physical changes occur during this period. Most will show up during the first six weeks of postpartum, but some will occur later, or continue for a longer time. Basically, all the changes begun by pregnancy are now reversed. The uterus and breasts will undergo the most obvious transformation, but there are other physical and emotional changes as well.

Within six weeks, the uterus will shrink from its post-delivery weight of about two pounds to about two ounces. This involution can cause cramps that will probably be more noticeable during breast-feeding. A heavier vaginal flow may also occur at this time. (This bleeding (or lochia) can continue for as long as six weeks). Although uncomfortable, the uterine contractions and flow are healthy signs of recovery. Pelvic Tilts may help reduce the discomfort.

This is an excerpt from *Your Fit Pregnancy Book* by Nell Weaver, copyright 1984. Published by Anderson World Books, it is now in bookstores.

The breasts have increased in size during pregnancy in preparation for breast-feeding. Colostrum has sometimes leaked from the breast during the last months, and by the third day after delivery, the milk supply has usually been produced. This process may cause painful engorgement that can be relieved by cold packs, warm showers, good bra support and, if you choose to do so, by nursing your baby. If you're breast-feeding, exercises for the arms and shoulders can reduce the pain of breast tenderness, and sore or cracked nipples will respond to the air, to gentle heat treatments (a blow dryer can be marvelous) and to ice packs. Ask your doctor or a friend who has breast-fed for additional treatment suggestions.

Don't expect the weight you gained in pregnancy to disappear right after delivery. The total weight of the baby, the amniotic fluid and the placenta will rarely be more than 12 pounds. In addition to the reduced weight of your uterus, you'll lose an additional two to three pounds of fluid. The rest of the weight will still be there, hanging in fatty tissue around the abdomen, waist, buttocks and thighs. In short, you have a lot of exercising to do! Breast-feeding should not interfere with your resolve to get your trim and healthy body back. You can eat the nutritious, wholesome diet necessary for breast-feeding and still have a diet compatible with your weight loss goal. A continued emphasis on posture and exercise, however, does play a crucial role in the postpartum recovery. And starting a moderate program, as soon as your body and your doctor agree that it's sensible to begin, will do wonders for your appearance and your morale. As in pregnancy, adequate rest plays an essential role at this time, so don't overdo your exercise; nor should you deny your body the nourishing effects of stretching exercises and a simple aerobic activity like walking.

Resuming a more strenuous activity such as running, aerobic dancing, lap swimming, racquetball, tennis, and so on, can be started as soon as you and your doctor agree you're ready. Start slowly and don't expect to be back to your pre-pregnancy performance levels within the first three months of postpartum. Don't create unrealistic goals and don't begrudge yourself for "lost" training time. That time wasn't lost; you stayed as fit as you could during your pregnancy and produced a new, healthy baby!

Most women continue to wear loose-fitting clothing during the fourth trimester. Although you may feel like giving them to Goodwill and having a joyous celebration, your maternity clothes may once again come in handy. If you are contemplating a new wardrobe, choose loose, classical styles that can be belted later when your body is smaller and firmer. If you're breast-feeding, buy dresses and blouses that button in the front. Simple, tailored shirtdresses are a good buy. For more casual wear, many women prefer a blouse and a wrap skirt, or a loose-fitting shirt worn over their maternity jeans. Choose clothing appropriate to your lifestyle, and remember that comfort is essential during the fourth trimester.

The emotional changes that occur during postpartum are as varied as the women experiencing them. Your partner will also be adapting to rapid change during this period, so be prepared to discuss any problems, doubts or fears as they occur. These feelings are perfectly natural for both of you, and for you especially, because of the hormonal changes that occur after delivery.

Not all of your concerns will be restricted to the immediate needs of your baby; even a second- or third-time mother is not immune. If you're planning to return to full-time work outside the home, you may feel guilty. If you've quit a job to become a full-time mom, you may be having second thoughts. You may wonder if you'll ever be slim again, or if your partner or other men will ever think you're attractive or "sexy." The worries accompanying your decision can lead to emotional stress. But you can avoid this stress by sharing your concerns with a close friend or counselor. In short, you are adjusting to one of the major events of your life. A trusted relative (for emotional support) or a paid household worker (for reducing your work load) can greatly help both of you adjust to the first weeks' demands in your life with a new baby. This extra help may seem like a luxury, but it will increase chances for a quicker recovery period.

The fitness skills you practiced in pregnancy should assist you in postpartum. Having learned to listen to your body during pregnancy, your body will carry over. The signals it gave you during pregnancy when it needed nourishment, rest and exercise will still be recognizable. You should listen to the cues and respond appropriately and quickly, just as you did in pregnancy. The baby will sometimes interfere with your ability to respond immediately to your personal needs, but remember that successful mothering is always a challenge to your physical and emotional stamina—and a new baby demands an especially fit mother!

POSTPARTUM: THE EXERCISES

These exercises are divided into three stages, each stage progressively more difficult. During the second or third stage, you will probably want to begin a simple aerobic exercise as well, such as walking. Adequate sleep and rest should also play an integral part in your postpartum recovery. Maintain correct posture during all your activities.

STAGE ONE

These exercises can be performed safely in bed or on the floor during the first two to three weeks after delivery. If you've had a cesarean delivery, ask your doctor which ones you can safely do.

Test For Recti Muscles Separation

1. Lie on your back, knees bent and pillows under head and shoulders. Place your hands on your abdomen.
2. Exhale, tuck in your chin and slowly lift head and shoulders. Keep breathing and see if you feel a soft, bulging spot in your abdomen. If so, the muscles have separated.
3. If you think the muscles have split, consult your doctor for confirmation and limit your exercise program to the rehabilitation exercise and to exercises that do not strain the abdominals.

Recti Muscles Rehabilitation

If your recti muscles have separated, this exercise should be the heart of your exercise program during the first few weeks after delivery. Consult your doctor before doing any other abdominal strengtheners.

1. Lie on your back with knees bent, feet comfortably apart. Use a pillow under your head and shoulders for comfort. Place your hands on your abdomen.
2. Exhale, lift your head and shoulders and use your hands to "encourage" the muscles of the abdomen to join. Hold for a few seconds. Release and repeat.

Hint: Be patient. Time and exercise will make it work.

Benefits: Encourages rehabilitation of the recti muscles, strengthening the abdominal wall.

Pelvic Floor Squeeze

1. Lie in a comfortable position.

2. Exhale, contract the muscles of the pelvic floor—the vaginal, urethal and anal sphincters. Squeeze them in and up. Hold for a few seconds, release. Repeat five times.

Variation: The squeeze can be done with Abdominal Lifts, Pelvic Tilts, and by stopping and starting the urinal flow.

Hint: Don't be discouraged if the pelvic floor seems unresponsive. Daily practice, begun on the first day after delivery, is the answer, but be patient and don't overwork the pelvic floor by doing "too much, too soon."

Benefit: Conditions pelvic floor.

Pelvic Tilts

1. Lie on your back with knees bent and feet comfortably apart and parallel.

2. Exhale, contract the buttocks and press the lower back into the bed or floor. Hold for a few seconds, release. Repeat five times.

Pelvic Tilts

Let your baby help you get back into shape!

Hint: Keep the face soft. Place your baby on your tummy for a partner exercise!

Benefit: Reduces lower back tension.

Mom's Stretch

1. Lie on your back with legs extended. Stretch the arms straight back. Place the feet together.

2. Exhale, stretch the right arm, then the left arm. Release.

3. Exhale, point the toes and stretch the legs away from your arms, and the arms away from the legs. Flatten the lower back on the bed or floor. Keep the face and neck relaxed. Hold for a few seconds. Release and repeat.

Variation: Do Mom's Stretch with the heels extended instead of the toes.

Hint: This is a marvelous stretch for a new mother as long as she keeps her pelvis in proper alignment by flattening the lower back.

Benefits: Reduces overall fatigue and body tension.

Mom's Stretch

Do Mom's Stretch while you're lying in bed before nursing your baby.

STAGE TWO

These exercises can usually be started within a month after a vaginal delivery.

Leg Lifts I

1. Lie on your back with knees bent, feet slightly apart and parallel. Arms at your sides. Press the lower back down.

2. Exhale, bring the left knee to the chest. Exhale, push the heel to the ceiling, straightening the leg. Hold for a few seconds, release the knee to the chest, then bring the foot to the floor. Reverse and repeat cycle several times.

Variation: When this becomes easy, bring the feet together and lift them as one leg.

Hint: Keep the lower back and the leg flat on the floor.

Benefits: Tones abdominals, stretches legs, reduces lower-back tension.

Hip Roll

1. Lie on your back with knees bent, feet slightly apart and parallel. Extend the arms perpendicular to your torso.

2. Exhale, roll the knees and left hip to the right. Exhale, reverse. Repeat cycle several times.

Variation: When this roll is easy, do it with the knees drawn into the chest and the feet off the floor.

Hint: Keep the shoulders down while you roll the hips.

Benefits: Tones waist, relieves lower-back tension.

Hip Roll

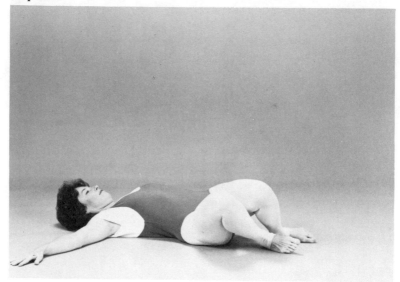

Do the hip roll with your feet on the floor.

STAGE THREE

Stage Three exercises can be started whenever most of the exercises in Stage Two become comfortable.

Triangle

1. Stand with the feet parallel and three to 3¹/₂ feet apart. Extend the arms horizontally to the floor. Turn the left foot in 30 degrees, the right leg out 90 degrees. The heel of the right foot points toward the middle of the left foot.

2. Exhale, move the hips to the left, and stretch the trunk to the right. Hold the right leg and stretch the left arm up. Keep the shoulders in line with the right knee. Tuck the right buttock under and lift the left pelvic bone back. Hold for a few seconds with straight legs. Release and reverse.

Hint: Don't allow the chest and abdomen to fall toward the floor. Don't try to take your hand to the floor; instead, see if you can keep the shoulders in line with the knees and the chest expanded.

Benefits: Tones legs, loosens hips and back.

Triangle

Your hips go to the left, and your torso stretches from the hips to the right.

Leg Release

1. Lie on your back with feet together.

2. Inhale, lift the legs up. Exhale, slowly lower the legs, trying to stop three times on the way down. Repeat several times.

Leg Release

Slowly bring your legs down, stopping three times as you go—tough, but great for shrinking that tummy!

Hint: Keep breathing and don't overarch the lower back. If this exercise causes too much strain, wait until the abdominals are a little stronger before doing it regularly.

Benefit: Strengthens the abdominals.

Hip Opener

1. Lie on your back with feet together, arms perpendicular to your sides.

2. Inhale, lift the right leg and turn the right toes out. Exhale, lower the right leg to the side, keeping the left shoulder down. Inhale as you lift up and change legs.

Variation: See if you can hold the right foot or leg with your right hand while you move it to the floor.

Hint: Keep the left buttock and the back of the left thigh pressed into the floor as the opposite leg goes down. If you allow the opposite buttock to lift up, the hips and inner thighs won't receive the maximum benefits of the stretch.

Benefits: Tones the inner thigh, stretches the entire leg, loosens the hips.

Hip Opener

Slowly lower the leg to the floor.

STAGE FOUR

When these exercises have become familiar and relatively comfortable, you can proceed to more challenging ones, such as those in *The Runner's World Stretching Book*.

BIBLIOGRAPHY

Adams, Catherine F. *Nutritive Value of American Foods* (Agriculture Handbook No. 456), Washington, D.C.: Agricultural Research Service, USDA, 1975.

Badalamenti, Rosalyn T. and Diane Klein. *Eating Right For Two*. New York: Ballantine Books, 1983.

Black, Helen, ed., *The Berkeley Co-op Food Book,* Palo Alto, CA: Bull Publishing, 1980.

Breast-feeding: Nature's Way to Feed Your Baby. Center For Science In The Public Interest, 1755 S St., NW, Washington, D.C. 20009, 1978.

Breast-feeding Your Baby, Ross Laboratories, Columbus, OH, 43216, 1981.

Brody, Jane. *Jane Brody's Guide To Personal Health*. New York: Avon, 1982.

Brody, Jane. *Jane Brody's Nutrition Book*. New York: W.W. Norton, 1981.

Castle, Sue. *The Complete New Guide to Preparing Baby Foods*. New York: Bantam Books, 1983.

Cohl, Vicki. *Science Experiments You Can Eat*. Philadelphia: J.B. Lippincott, 1973.

Croft, Karen B. *The Good For Me Cookbook*. 741 Maplewood Place, Palo Alto, CA 94303, 1971.

DeMoss, Virginia. *Runner's World Vitamin Book*. Mountain View, CA: Runner's World Books, 1982.

Deutsch, Ronald M. *The Fat Counter Guide*. Palo Alto, CA: Bull Publishing, 1978.

Eating Right For Your Baby. Maternal and Child Health Branch, California Dept. of Health Services, 714 P St., Sacramento, CA 95814.

Favorite Junk Food Alternatives. B.E.A.N.S., c/o Mrs. Virginia Jouris, 1632 Green Valley Road, Danville, CA 94526.

Feeding Recommendations For Healthy Infants. Missouri Division of Health, Dept. of Social Services, P.O. Box 570, Jefferson City, MO 65102, 1982.

The Feingold Handbook. Feingold Association of the United States. Drawer A-G, Holtsville, NY 11742, 1982.

Food and Nutrition Board, National Academy of Sciences — National Research Council. *Recommended Dietary Allowances*. Ninth Ed., Washington, D.C.: National Academy of Sciences, 1980.

Food For Little People. Berkeley Health Dept., 2180 Milvia, Berkeley, CA 94704.

From Pregnancy To Parenthood. Ross Laboratories, Columbus, OH 43216, 1981.

Goldbeck, Nikki. *As You Eat So Your Baby Grows*. Ceres Press, Box 87 Dept. D, Woodstock, NY 12498, 1980.

Goodwin, Mary T. and Gerry Pollen. *Creative Food Experiences For Children*. Washington, D.C.: Center For Science In The Public Interest, 1980.

Hausman, Patricia. *Jack Sprat's Legacy: The Science and Politics of Fat & Cholesterol*. New York: Richard Marek Publishers, 1981.

Hill, Reba Michels. *Breast Feeding*. American Academy of Pediatrics, P.O. Box 1034, Evanston, IL 60204, 1981.

How To Formula-feed Your Baby. Ross Laboratories, Columbus, OH 43216.

Jacobson, Michael F. *Nutrition Scoreboard*. New York: Avon Books, 1975.

Jacobson, Michael, Bonnie F. Liebman and Greg Moyer. Salt: *The Brand Name Guide To Sodium Content*. Washington, D.C.: Center For Science In The Public Interest, 1983.

Kenda, Margaret Elizabeth, and Phyllis S. Williams. *The Natural Baby Food Cookbook*. New York: Avon Books, 1972.

Kiester, Edwin Jr., and Sally Valente Kiester. *Better Homes and Gardens New Baby Book*. New York: Bantam Books, 1979.

Kraus, Barbara. *The Barbara Kraus 1983 Sodium Guide To Brand Names & Basic Foods*. New York: Signet, 1982.

Kreutler, Patricia A. *Nutrition in Perspective*. Englewood Cliffs, NJ: Prentice-Hall, 1980.

Labuza, Theodore P., and A. Elizabeth Sloan. *Contemporary Nutrition Controversies*. St. Paul, MN: West Publishing, 1979.

Labuza, Theodore P. *The Nutrition Crisis*. St. Paul, MN: West Publishing, 1975.

La Leche League International. *The Womanly Art of Breastfeeding*. Franklin Park, IL: La Leche League, 1981.

Lansky, Vicki. *Feed Me! I'm Yours*. New York: Bantam Books, 1979.

Lansky, Vicki. *The Taming Of The C.A.N.D.Y. Monster*. New York: Bantam Books, 1978.

Lappe, Frances Moore. *Diet For A Small Planet*. 2nd edition. New York: Ballantine Books, 1983.

Mayer, Jean. *A Diet For Living*. New York: Simon & Schuster, 1975.

My Baby's First Food. Division of Agricultural Sciences, University of California, Berkeley, CA 94720, 1980.

Nutrition Action Newsletter. Center For Science In The Public Interest, 1755 S St. NW, Washington, D.C. 20009.

Nutrition, Growth and Development During Your Baby's First Year. Ross Laboratories, Columbus, OH 43216, 1981.

Nutritioning Parents (newsletter). P.O. Box 13825, Atlanta, GA 30324.

Pediatric Nutrition Handbook. American Academy of Pediatrics, P.O. Box 1034, Evanston, IL 60204, 1979.

Prenatal Care, American Medical Association, 535 N. Dearborn St., Chicago, IL 60610, 1978.

Pritikin, Nathan. *The Pritikin Program For Diet & Exercise.* New York: Bantam Books, 1979.

Pryor, Karen. *Nursing Your Baby.* New York: Simon & Schuster, 1973.

Spock, Benjamin. *Baby and Child Care.* New York: Simon & Schuster, 1976.

United States Senate Select Committee on Nutrition and Human Needs, *Dietary Goals For the United States,* Washington, D.C.: U.S. Government Printing Office 20402, 1977.

USDA. *Nutrition and Your Health: Dietary Guidelines for Americans.* Superintendent of Documents, U.S. Government Printing Office, Washington, D.C. 20402.

What Shall I Feed My Baby? USDA Program Aid No. 1281, Superintendent of Documents, U.S. Government Printing Office, Washington, D.C. 20402, 1981.

Wurtman, Judith J. *Eating Your Way Through Life.* New York: Raven Press.